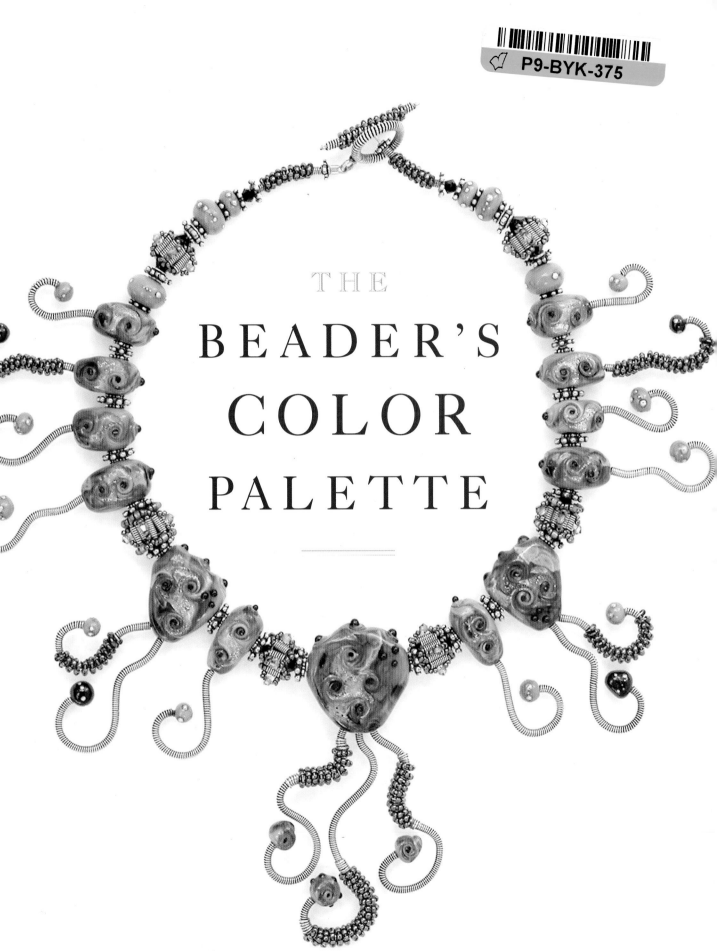

THE
BEADER'S
COLOR
PALETTE

THE
BEADER'S
COLOR
PALETTE

20 CREATIVE PROJECTS
220 INSPIRED COMBINATIONS FOR
BEADED AND GEMSTONE JEWELRY

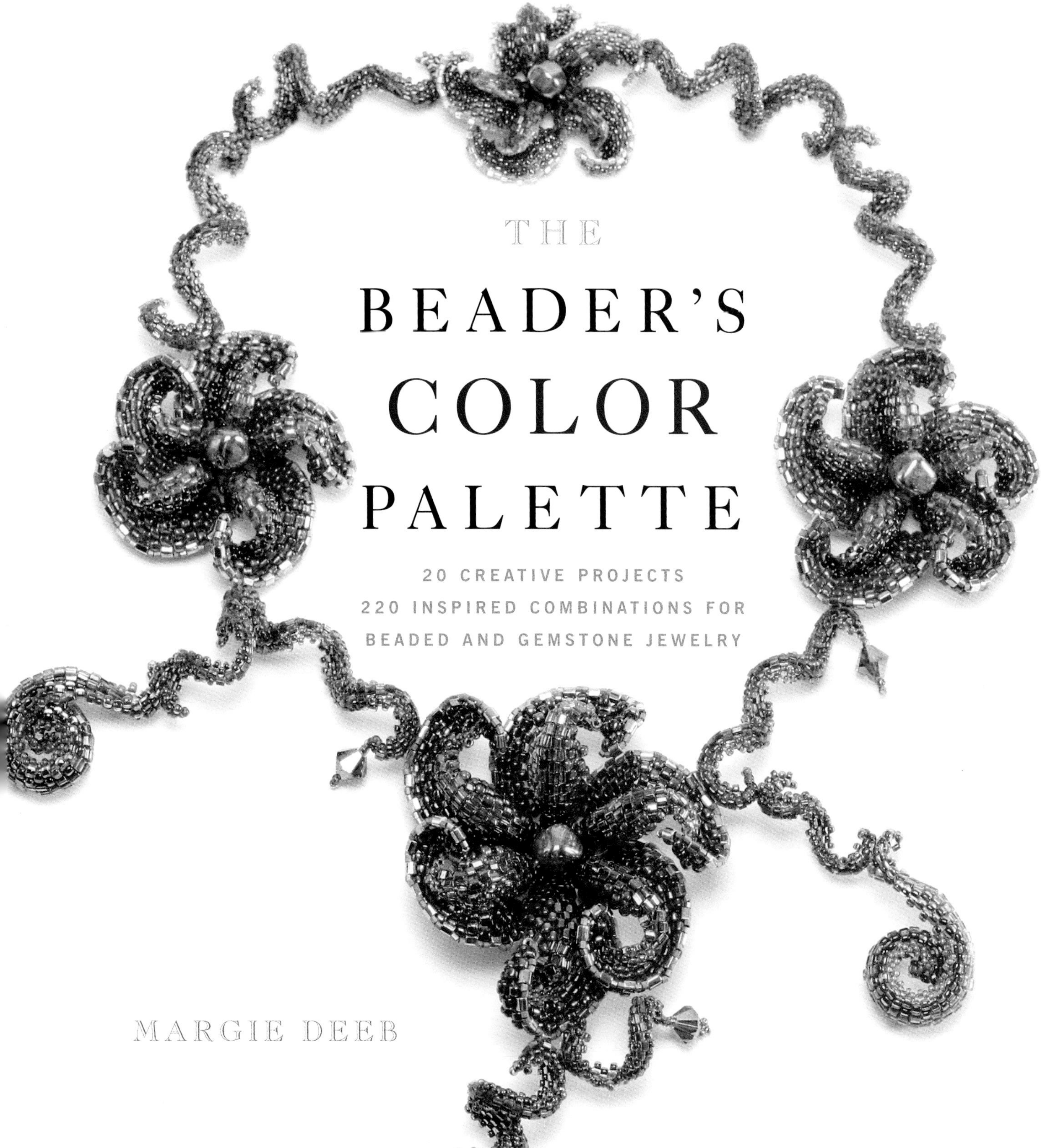

MARGIE DEEB

WATSON-GUPTILL PUBLICATIONS

NEW YORK

Please visit my website for color and beading inspiration, books, patterns, and more:
www.margiedeeb.com
or e-mail me at: margie@margiedeeb.com

Executive Editor: Joy Aquilino
Editor: Martha Moran
Designer: Chin-Yee Lai
Art Director: Timothy Hsu
Production Director: Alyn Evans
Copy Editor: Daryl Brower

First published in 2008 by
Watson-Guptill Publications,
Crown Publishing Group,
a division of Random House Inc., New York
www.crownpublishing.com
www.watsonguptill.com

ISBN-13: 978-0-8230-0474-4
ISBN-10: 0-8230-0474-0

Library of Congress Cataloging-in-Publication Number: 2007936519

Printed in China
First printing, 2008
3 4 5 6 7 8 9 / 16 15 14 13 12 11 10

Overleaf: *Pinwheel Garden*
Paulette Baron
Photograph by Brownwen Sexton

For Darren,

whose vision, support, and encouragement made this possible.

ACKNOWLEDGMENTS

I gratefully acknowledge the following people who played an essential part in making this book whole:

The artists whose work appears on these pages for generously sharing their talent and expertise.

Robin Atkins, SaraBeth Cullinan, Kristy Nijenkamp, Mary Hicklin, Thom Atkins, and Heidi Kummli for the time, talent, and expertise they contributed to creating projects.

Frieda Bates for all her expertise, skill, and gracious generosity.

Allison O'Neill for her generosity, support, and photographic contribution.

Ken Alexander, Steven Ford, and Francisco Silva for their generous photographic contributions.

My editor Joy Aquilino for her invaluable ideas, feedback, and encouragement.

Darren Nelsen, for his support, encouragement, patience, and love.

GeoMagical Frenzy
by Jeanette Cook
Right angle weave, peyote, netting,
and indebele stitch
Lampwork by Gail Crossman Moore,
Michelle Waldren, and John Winter

TABLE OF CONTENTS

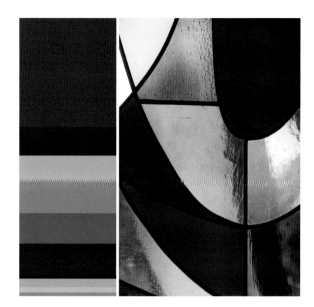

INTRODUCTION

Our world offers up an endless deluge of color inspiration. The purpose of *The Beader's Color Palette* is to help you identify and harvest those color combinations that transport you into ecstatic wonder.

The 220 palettes presented in these pages are a result of time-travel, globe-trotting, deep-sea diving, and rainforest trekking, mixed with intuition, passion, and a lifetime of color study. The hardest part for me was stopping at 220. There are thousands more where these came from!

In creating extraordinary color combinations, color itself has done half the work. It comes to you in all its splendor asking that you participate, opening yourself to its radiant dialect. Sharpen your perception. Answer its shifts with shifts in your self. Through your presence, color asks that you become a profoundly nuanced observer.

With all your senses awake and humming, you embark on the remaining half of the effort. Use the presented palettes exactly as they are. Or position yourself squarely on one and take a leap, deepening one shade, or adding another. Experiment with them. Play with them. Let them speak—or sing—to you. And listen to them. Hear each unique harmony.

Color is so many things: an energy, a language, a means to discover yourself, a vehicle for expression, pure magic. Above all, color is, and should be, fun.

So dive in and let it be. The fun has just begun.

An array of reds, pinks, and purples from a stained glass window inspire a rich bead palette.

HOW TO READ THE PALETTES

In these pages I have presented 220 groups of color swatches that combine to create color palettes. The palettes illustrate specific colors, how they interact with each other, and proportional amounts of each color to be used.

Figure 1

DB-287 transmits a myriad of colors because of its AB surface finish. In the flat expanses of ink used to depict the palettes, it is represented like this.

The color swatches in each palette are printed in CMYK ink formulas that approximate Delica bead colors as closely as possible. Delica beads are Japanese cylindrical seed beads available in most bead stores and on the Web. Because they are identified by number, they are my choice for specifying exact hues and finishes. For example, the designation "DB-287" refers to Delica bead #287, a lined brown topaz with an AB finish. It is not necessary to use Delicas for these palettes. Use any brand or size bead or gemstone you prefer to match the color swatches and descriptions.

A bead's exact hue cannot be accurately reproduced in ink on a two-dimensional surface for several reasons. The surface finish of a bead reflects varying degrees of color, both the colors of the surrounding beads and the environment. Highly reflective beads reflect more light and less color. Less reflective beads display more color and less light. This cannot be illustrated with ink on paper.

Because the swatches are printed in flat ink colors, the metallic, iris, rainbow, and Aurora Borealis (AB) finishes cannot be accurately represented. However, an attempt has been made to depict their appearance (figure 1). Look at the actual beads to see their true finish and how they work together with other members of the palette.

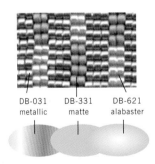

DB-031 metallic   DB-331 matte   DB-621 alabaster

Three different gold Delica® beads represented in a photo and in palette form.

Each palette suggests approximate amounts of specific colors to be combined. Accordingly, each color swatch within each palette is shaped proportionately. The largest area of color is considered the dominant color, and is listed first. Use more of this dominant color than any of the others in the palette (figure 2).

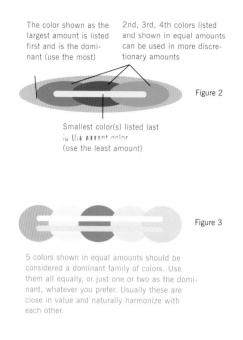

The color shown as the largest amount is listed first and is the dominant (use the most)

2nd, 3rd, 4th colors listed and shown in equal amounts can be used in more discretionary amounts

Figure 2

Smallest color(s) listed last is the accent color (use the least amount)

Figure 3

5 colors shown in equal amounts should be considered a dominant family of colors. Use them all equally, or just one or two as the dominant, whatever you prefer. Usually these are close in value and naturally harmonize with each other.

Sometimes many colors are shown in the same sized shape (figure 3). This indicates that there is no one dominant color. Use the whole group as a dominant family. Where smaller amounts of color are presented in a swatch, use smaller amounts in your work.

Delica numbers are sequenced in the same order as their respective swatch colors: back to front, left to right, and top to bottom (figure 4).

Use the Delica Cross-Reference on pages 187–188 to locate all palettes in the book containing a specific Delica bead color.

1 2 3 4 5 6

Figure 4

Delica® numbers are sequenced in the same order as their respective swatch colors: from back to front, left to right, and top to bottom. DELICAS: (1)DB-651, (2)DB-233, (3)DB-749, (4)DB-210, (5)DB-001, (6)DB-800

CREATING PALETTES

You're going about your day when you stumble upon a surprising combination of colors. Stopped in your tracks your heart beats faster, your imagination soars. You want to use this scheme—this sublime, wonder-filled color harmony—in your beadwork. But where do you go from here? Can you simply copy the colors as you see them? Sometimes it's possible; follow the proportions and you have a winning, ready-made palette.

Most of the time however, it's not that simple. Working in beads, a premixed medium with a limited range of colors, you won't be able to match the colors exactly as you see them. You must make adjustments to hue, value, intensity, and luminosity.

Selecting the Main Colors

First you need to determine the overriding colors you'll be working with. If it's a very busy image or one containing many colors, squint your eyes, letting details blur, so you can recognize main masses of color.

Figure 1

Figure 2

Working with the photo of trees in the mist (figure 1), it's easy to determine the four main color families without squinting. In the sky we see light pinks and orange-yellows; in the earth we see dark yellow-greens leaning toward brown; the silhouetted trees and fence are a rich warm brown. (Use whatever medium you prefer to work out the colors before beginning your final project. You can spread out tubes of beads or swatches of colored paper, use markers and pencils, or work on a computer.)

Now zero in on color nuances. The sky presents countless shades. The smooth gradation begins with a pinkish lavender at the top then gradates to light pink. The palest pink slides into a white and then into a shimmering yellow in the bottom half on the right. There are many shades of brown and green in the grass.

Too many colors within a palette become visually confusing, so I limit my selection to eight or less. I can add more later, if I choose. To the left are the four main colors alongside four additional tones (figure 2) that I find the most powerful in the photo.

This palette, though accurate, doesn't speak to me like the colors in the photo. Time for tweaking.

Re-examine the Image and Tweak

Let's revisit the photo to determine what makes the color scheme sublime. Note the graceful movement of color within the gradations. Pinkish lavender shifts imperceptibly into a more pure pink, which slides into pale pink, then into white, and into yellow, and so on. By simply using a few of the colors in those gradations I can't achieve the elegant movement that is inherent in the photo. I am limited by my medium of beads. Unless I'm weaving many rows of seed beads into a tapestry of gradations, I accept that this graceful movement of color will not be part of my final piece.

Part of the beauty of the color scheme in the photo above is the appearance of luminosity. In part, this is a result of the gradations, but it is more a result of the colors' lightness and darkness in relation to each other. Looking at the orange and yellow I've pulled, I see they don't look as bright as they do in the photo, so I'll choose to lighten them.

The green from the photo is quite dark and very brown. I may choose to use a deep green for an accent, but I will achieve more luminosity if I lighten and brighten the green as well (figure 3).

Figure 3

Proportions

Another factor that makes the photo on page 11 beautiful is the proportions of colors—the amount of each color relative to the other. I like to experiment with the proportions, changing the dominant, secondary, and accent colors until I arrive at proportions that feel are balanced and whole (figure 3). Determining that balance takes a leap of faith. Trust yourself if you are new at it. Look at the proportions several times, returning to them after a few minutes or hours, and from different angles. Go with what feels and looks right.

This exercise (right) confirms that I want to use the lavender-pink family for the dominant color palette, as in the photo. While the other proportions work, lavender-pinks are what make the palette so unusual, so I decided to emphasize them. Notice that although the photo contains white, I've omitted it. I think the pale pink will have more impact if it is the lightest color. I've reduced the amount of green and brown so they become accents, thus giving the lavender-pinks more voice. Here is my final palette (figure 4).

Figure 4

Notice how different the palette looks when the dominant color or dominant color family is changed.

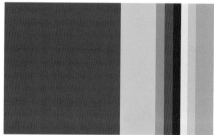

Pink family as dominant

Green family as dominant

Brown family as dominant

Yellow-orange family as dominant

Choosing Your Materials

From what I've learned with the flat color swatches, I've selected a possible bead palette. Even though there's no true lavender in the photo's color scheme, lavender (in the form of light amethyst) works beautifully with the beads I've chosen, so I'll stray from the original palette and include it. I've also included a couple of yellow possibilities, one transparent and one opaque. Peridot is a light yellow-green, and nothing like it appears in the photo. But I see how well it contrasts and harmonizes with the other beads, so I've invited it to join the palette. Because beads and gemstones are not the exact colors of the flat swatches, I will continue experimenting with proportions, just as I did with the color swatches. I'll also consider how the different finishes interact with each other.

A. amethyst
B. 11/o seed beads
C. Delica bead 072
D. pressed glass
E. rose quartz
F. pressed glass
G. pressed glass
H. Delica bead 071
I. faceted citrine
J. aragonite
K. 11/o seed beads
L. tourmaline
M. peridot
N. mahogany obsidian
O. carnelian

PALETTES

&

PROJECTS

The palettes are a jumping off point—a springboard to using color in a way that reflects you. Be flexible, give your curiosity and wonder free reign. Choose a palette from these pages and throw yourself into it. Use it as is, in the suggested proportions, or add more of a certain color, or darken a shade. You can also add a handful of similar colors to broaden the color family. The trick to making color relationships work is to combine your knowledge of color principles and your intuition. If you don't have a working knowledge of color theory, start by observing your world carefully, looking for what speaks to you and why. And above all, experiment! Play with color in many mediums—colored paper, fabric, pencils, paint—whatever methods you desire to deepen your intimacy with color. As you build your relationship with color, you'll begin to sense what works and what doesn't. And color will begin working with you.

Diane Guzman
Glass cabochons and beads on
handmade footstool
Photograph by David Guzman

Python Rib Necklace
by Mary Hicklin
Snake rib bones, hand-beaded leather,
antique trade beads, snake beads
Photograph by Melinda Holden

THE ELEMENTS

Robin Atkins finishes off
Air Currents with the tinkling of bells
at the ends of strands of vintage
pressed glass, pearls, sterling, and a
lampworked focal bead.

Storms provide endless color drama.

AIR

Air symbolizes the winds of change and forces of transcendence. In the Tarot and in ancient magic, air is represented by a sword, and speaks to us of freedom, wisdom, and power.

The color palettes for air range from breeze-like pastel wisps to muted storm-gray rhapsodies.

More important than color itself is how the beads interact with light. Choose luminous stones that appear to dance with light, or glow from within. Materials that are transparent, translucent, or have an iridescent finish form the basis of the ephemeral air palette.

In her organic, curving style,
Margie Deeb surrounds blue
chalcedony with ivory and
shades of purple and sky-blue.

1. The Wisdom of Raphael

Violet tones create a luxurious backdrop for the ethereal glow of the glamorous coral and peach accents inspired by the photo above. Each Delica displays a different surface finish, augmenting the inherent drama of the combination. Include amethyst with peach-colored freshwater pearls. **Delicas: DB-923, DB-694, DB-235, DB-1479**

2. Mistral Wind

Shimmering violet is the gust of cold, northerly wind from the southern coast of France. Light sky blues, cream, and pale lavender-gray offer their delicacy to this atmospheric palette. Try these colors in amethyst, blue chalcedony, and mother-of-pearl. **Delicas: DB-906, DB-240, DB-203, DB-080, DB-1537**

As luminous as the sun through the clouds, opalite (also called "sea opal") is a man-made, translucent, milky-colored glass with blue undertones. Its color and sparkle make it a quintessential member of the air palette. Necklace by Margie Deeb
Photograph by Haigwood Studios

THE ELEMENTS

SUGGESTED AIR
PALETTE MATERIALS

Transparent
amethyst
ametrine
clear quartz
citrine
tanzanite

Translucent
rose quartz
iolite
labradorite
lavender fluorite

blue agate
blue lace agate
prehnite

Iridescent
rainbow moonstone
iridescent
freshwater pearls

Amulets & Symbols
feathers
sword

3. Breath of Heaven

Subdued and misty, this classic antique-like palette brings to mind Victorian lace and porcelain. Soft, powdery tones create the ambiance of a romantic, bygone era. Matte rose, the strongest color, boosts vitality and keeps the scheme from becoming too melancholy. **Delicas: DB-361, DB-240, DB-381, DB-1457, DB-800**

4. Iridescence and Light

Reminiscent of the hues Marcia DeCoster uses in her French Rococo palette on page 41, these colors and finishes (crystal AB and opaque AB) float like gossamer veils in the breeze. Be sure to use 24kt gold beads, not silver-lined gold beads, which are too bright for this airy scheme. **Delicas: DB-1500, DB-082, DB-083, DB-031**

18

5. Shimmering Sylph

This complex group of colors lifted from the photo below requires carefully planned proportions and placement. Blues dominate, with only wisps of the pale lemon, peach, and crystal AB. In gemstones, blue chalcedony, citrine, rainbow moonstone, and labradorite create a similar palette. **Delicas: DB-085, DB-113, DB-1471, DB-622, DB-051**

Transparent and translucent hues in the sky create ethereal, magical palettes.

The layers of cleavage planes within labradorite create iridescent glimmers, called "labradorescence," that refract light back and forth. Blue dyed chalcedony enhances these small universes full of color.
Necklace by Margie Deeb

6. Mists of Zephyr

Gentle breezes of light and color whisper through this ethereal, gauzy color scheme. Transparent luster and lined crystal AB finishes tinge the palette with sparkling highlights. **Delicas: DB-057, DB-1473, DB-083, DB-1479**

7. Gale Force

A tempest of stormy grays creates a perfect scheme for jewelry to match a simple black dress, especially if you sparkle it up with silver. Desaturated, windy blue (DB-376) adds a sophisticated hint of color, reminiscent of tanzanite. **Delicas: DB-301, DB-376, DB-381, DB-209**

8. Sirroco

Yellow and topaz AB represent the hot, dry, dust-laden wind that blows from the Sahara Desert across North Africa. Accent these warm tones with a shimmering sky blue AB. All finishes are highly reflective. Consider including topaz, citrine, amber, and turquoise. **Delicas: DB-100, DB-233, DB-203, DB-076**

Gemstones and glass beads of the air palette

Black, representing the aftermath of
fire, injects even more drama into
the heat of fire palettes.

FIRE

Symbolized by the staff in ancient magic and the
Tarot, Fire inspires motivation, passion, and car-
ing. While it has the ability to create and make
stronger by forging, fire can also destroy by
breaking down and consuming.

These energetic palettes are hot and dry. Their textures are
smooth or tessellated, and their movement is active—a fast
and rhythmic staccato. They burst like a supernova or blaze
like a bonfire. Fire energy is so dynamic it creates forceful
palettes that simultaneously startle and mesmerize.

Sunny
Orange flames radiate like the sun
in this bead-embroidered pendant
by Frieda Bates.
Swarovski crystals, braided nylon
and cotton strap

Robin Atkins forged a *Ring of Fire*,
with a blazing bracelet of flames.
Peyote stitch, glass seed beads

9. Heart of Passion

Shades of red accented with 24kt gold combine to give this passionate palette the feel of a romantic valentine. Include gemstones of red agate, red coral, red aventurine, and either citrine or gold, or both. **Delicas: DB-296, DB-654, DB-757, DB-031**

10. Candleflame

A warm, glimmering trio begins with two oranges: transparent and silver lined, to form a foundation of heat. Accents of gentle buttercup yellow flicker and flare. This simple, analogous scheme that generates a lot of heat can be created with carnelian and citrine. Finish it off with gold. **Delicas: DB-703, DB-045, DB-233**

11. Heart and Hearth

Warmth and subtle luster are the themes in this delicious scheme. Toasted amber brown (DB-115) glows with burnished orange, topaz and a softly glowing matte metallic 24kt yellow gold. Beiges and browns occur in natural mother-of-pearl. Mahogany obsidian, tigereye, and amber convey the warmth in gemstones. **Delicas: DB-115, DB-781, DB-651, DB-742, DB-331**

12. Blinking Embers

Both charcoal grays have a matte finish, so the highly contrasting oranges and the goldenrod appear even brighter, glowing like the tip of embers. Include hematite, carnelian, and citrine. A bold, daring palette that calls for clean lines and simple details. **Delicas: DB-301, DB-749, DB-1302, DB-722, DB-651**

13. Lambent Twilight

To appreciate the beauty of this palette, you need to see the beads' surface finishes. DB-913 and DB-914 are crystal-lined, so they shimmer, while the staid matte finish of the topaz (DB-742) calms the activity. Tension exists between the interaction of their movement, heightening the warmth. **Delicas: DB-913, DB-914, DB-742**

14. Burnished Sunflowers

What a fun trio of colors! Blazing matte yellow, goldenrod, and dark chocolate brown mimic the glory of a sunflower. The association is so apparent, you may have to weave a few bold blossoms with this palette. **Delicas: DB-751, DB-651, DB-734**

15. Dawn's First Rays

When yellow, pink and coral first emerge from night's dwindling violet, the world pauses with a hush. Articulate these light pearl colors with a streak of dark shimmering violet for an extraordinary array of tones. **Delicas: DB-232, DB-235, DB-236, DB-923**

16. Solar Winds

The stream of particles shooting out from the sun and sculpting the tails of comets could wear these highly charged and luxurious colors. This stellar complementary harmony asks for amethyst, carnelian, and citrine to propel it even higher. **Delicas: DB-161, DB-610 DB-073, DB-233**

In Margie Deeb's *Radiant Sun* earrings the gold emits fire energy from every facet.
Gold Czech fire polished beads
Instructions on pages 28 and 29

Gemstones and glass beads of the fire palette

Carnelian, tigereye, and gold form a
dramatic burst of fire energy.
Necklace by Margie Deeb
Photograph by Haigwood Studios

SUGGESTED FIRE PALETTE MATERIALS

Transparent	*Translucent*	*Opaque*	
citrine	red aventurine	red agate	black onyx
amber	carnelian	red coral	hematite
	garnet	red jade	obsidian
	sunstone (aventurine	red aventurine	gold
	feldspar)	tigereye	
			Amulets & Symbols
			staff

The blazing colors of the sun and its
glow make up the fire palette.

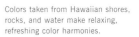

Colors taken from Hawaiian shores, rocks, and water make relaxing, refreshing color harmonies.

WATER

The playful side of water comes forth in Kimberley Price's *Flower Fairy* bracelet. Yellow undertones transform pure blues and greens into a tropical water palette.
Lampwork by Lezlie Winemaker Levitt
Glass seed beads in peyote stitch, right angle weave, spiral rope

Shoreline Fantasy (below) by SaraBeth Cullinan combines earth and water by embellishing a stone with beads of the water palette. Using a yellow-based green makes water scheme earthier.
Glass beads, pearls, peyote stitch
Photograph by Robert Still

> The Tarot represents this feminine energy as a cup or chalice, and from it we learn of transmutation and transformation, of joy, and of healing. The universal solvent, water—in time—will dissolve everything.
>
> Water's movement is fast and turbulent, or slow and serene. It progresses in repeated textures and patterns, and rounded curvilinear forms.

Transparent or translucent stones reflect the depth of water. Opaque stones and beads of the water palette must have a moist, reflective surface. Water designs can be as light as a spray coming off of a waterfall, or as heavy and substantial as the sea.

Harmonious tension is created by placing warm greens against cool blues and grays.

An extraordinary water palette is
inspired by this photo of Lake Louise.

Could there be a more perfect palette for
embellishing a mirror? Like a magical
reflecting pool, the rhythmic composition
and the blue-greens of the water palette lend
a magical quality to Tracey Rodgerson's
extraordinary bead-embroidered mirror.
Glass beads, fused glass cabochons

SUGGESTED WATER
PALETTE MATERIALS

Transparent
aquamarine
apatite
peridot

Translucent
green agate
blue agate
jade
fluorite
prehnite
serpentine
chalcedonies
   (dyed in the blue-green ranges)

Opaque
chrysocolla
chrysoprase
malachite
sodalite
lapis
amazonite
pearl
moonstone
sodalite

Amulets & Symbols
shells
starfish

Margie Deeb uses silver to unify dyed
chalcedony beads with amazonite, the
ultimate water palette gemstone.

17. The Ancient Mariner

Blown off course by a storm, the mariner in Coleridge's tale was faced with nothing but an endless expanse of these dulled blue-green tones. There the white albatross brought its light of hope which, unfortunately, was lost on the sailor but not on this palette. Creamy white (DB-883) lifts the color scheme out of melancholy and into cool, tranquil comfort. **Delicas: DB-377, DB-788, DB-792, DB-883**

18. Lady of the Lake

Through veils of emerald under silver starlight she works her magic. This array of clear greens, both warm and cool, casts a mesmerizing spell, especially when embellished with accents of silver. Toss in several shades of green aventurine dotted with amazonite. **Delicas: DB-275, DB-746, DB-237, DB-904, DB-1536, DB-032**

19. The Isle of Innisfree

Glimmering water colors sing the music of Innisfree, calling the "deep heart's core" to peace. Sparkling cobalt and sapphire pearl are the lake water lapping on the shore of opaque and shimmering greens. "Noon's purple" glows in a semi-matte, silver-lined alabaster finish. **Delicas: DB-285, DB-240, DB-663, DB-917, DB-1454, DB-694**

20. Sisters of the Caldron

The first two colors in this glamorous gathering bring to mind the peacock greens of chrysoprase. Pearlescent warm green (DB-691) flows into a misty mint, (DB-1506) whose finish hints at secrets beneath its AB surface. **Delicas: DB-918, DB-793, DB-691, DB-1506**

21. Koi Pond

A palette straight from the shubunkin-filled pond in our back yard. At 22-plus years old, the reigning koi, Goldie, is represented by luminous, silver-lined orange (DB-045) glistening like scales. In gemstones, try olive "jade," peridot, and banded red and white onyx. **Delicas: DB-011, DB-131, DB-371, DB-045**

22. The Mermaid's Rainbow

An ocean-dweller's dream, these iridescent, scale-like beads, each have an AB finish. Rapidly shifting light and color evoke the elusive mermaid whom sailors have sought for centuries. **Delicas: DB-859, DB-169, DB-079, DB-078, DB-1506**

23. Babbling Brook

While liquescent blues—dark, light,—warm, and cool—commingle to create a wash of calm, lavender introduces luxury to the flow. The palette exudes a buoyant tranquility. Include lapis lazuli, blue lace and blue agate, and light amethyst. **Delicas: DB-285, DB-257, DB-249, DB-787, DB-057**

24. The River Sea

A range of warm greens, some leaning strongly toward yellow, takes its inspiration form our world's most voluminous river, the Amazon. So much of the plant, animal, and human life it nourishes remains unknown or undiscovered—such is its intrigue. **Delicas: DB-011, DB-371, DB-917, DB-274, DB-908**

25. Undine Dream

Moving from oceanic, iridescent blue-violet (DB-165) through turquoise and warm greens, the water spirit's dream palette finishes in a shimmering, light, rainbow-finished blue. **Delicas: DB-165, DB-787, DB-746, DB-237, DB-057**

Gemstones and glass beads of the water palette

Frieda Bates Pecos River
by Frieda Bates
A rock with a natural hole through it
inspired the artist to craft this award-
winning necklace with an earth palette
of cool mountain grays.
Glass beads, stone, pewter, silver

Earth palettes can be cool, as are the
gray-blues of these mountains.

EARTH

> **Strong and solid, the element of earth is symbolized in the
> Tarot by the shield, which, when turned on its side, represents
> a platter of bounty and abundance. Earth energy resonates
> with authority, inspiration, and choice.**

This is the palette of trees and plants, the roots of which reach deep for
sustenance. It is also the palette of metals, which form in deep and hidden places. And it is the palette of rock and sand, and the soil blanketing
our planet.

Earth palettes run the gamut of temperature and texture. Rocks can
be hot and cold, smooth or rough. Soil can be moist; sand can be dry as
bone. Tree bark can be craggy and untouchable, or seemingly polished.

Earth energy can be represented with many irregular shapes and elements, or it can be one smooth, metallic, focal piece of substance.

Earth's abundant palette can include almost any kind of amulet
found in nature, from bones and feathers, dried seed pods and leaves to
twigs, animal teeth, and fossils. (See Mary Hicklin's necklace on page 79.)

SUGGESTED EARTH PALETTE MATERIALS

Browns & Golds	*Blacks & Grays*	*Greens & Blues*	serpentine	*Amulets & Symbols*
tigereye	hematite	amazonite	jasper	shells
jaspers & agates	obsidian	chrysoprase	unakite	bones & fossils
smokey quartz	black onyx	chrysocolla		seeds & pods
citrine	blue goldstone	turquoise	*Metals*	shield
feldspath		aventurine	copper	
African brown rhyolite		malachite	bronze	
		olivine	silver	
		tourmaline	gold	

Karen Lewis (*Klew*) uses a warm earth palette of tree and flora colors reminiscent of a stroll through a meadow in early spring. Freeform beadwork by Kathy Wood, using glass and stone to accent *Klew*'s polymer focal bead.

Complex woody browns and greens make substantial color palettes.

Betcey's Bear by Heidi Kummli. Myriad colors and amulets of the earth, from precious metal clay to stone, wood, and bone, combine in an elegant song of nature's abundant gifts.
Photograph by Heidi Kummli

26. Love Me Like Rock

Like a granite boulder, a solid foundation of cool gray gives solidity and weight to this scheme. Three matte finishes add to its substance, while an opaque pale blue ceylon (DB-1537) provides flecked highlights.
Delicas: DB-301, DB-377, DB-376, DB-1537

27. Tea in the Sahara

This palette is as warm as it is rich. Pull out tubes of these three colors and you'll feel the hot, dry sand. The three colors and surface finishes combine so easily you could use equal amounts of each for stunning results. Or try variations, changing the dominant color each time. **Delicas: DB-272, DB-764, DB-651**

28. Gnomes in the Loam

Mine these precious metallic beads into a sophisticated scheme, starting with galvanized copper (DB-461) for the dominant color. Use gunmetal gray (DB-001) liberally and accent with a tarnished silver color (DB-254), and a 24kt-gold plated finish. Because these are highly reflective, this palette creates sparkling results. If you want to reduce the glare, throw in matte black. **Delicas: DB-461, DB-001, DB-254, DB-031**

29. Painted Desert

Slowly and quietly the painted desert offers up its colorful nuances. Each hue merges into another, building a remarkable landscape. Linked together by their dusty softness, these other-worldly tones harmonize beautifully.
Delicas: DB-769, DB-1454, DB-1532, DB-1500

30. Of Moss and Stone

Blue is traditionally of water and sky. Here, because it is toned-down and darkened, it expresses the strong solidity of stone. Cool mossy greens lighten and brighten the overall effect. Include blue agate, grey moonstone or tanzanite, malachite, and serpentine green "jade." **Delicas: DB-278, DB-381, DB-275, DB-1484**

31. Painted Hills

This unusual and sophisticated harmony comes from the Painted Hills in Oregon. The gold is pale, yet shimmery, thanks to its silver lining and alabaster finish. Each member of the group is reflective, with grey (DB-081) emitting flashes of blue, pink, and green courtesy of an AB finish. **Delicas: DB-621, DB-116, DB-081, DB-1500**

32. Terrestrial Sentinels

Ancient trees stand guard, spreading their limbs across the sky, protecting us with their canopy of leaves. Three versions of coppery brown contrast against three very different shades of green, representing the majesty of these sentinels. **Delicas: DB-312, DB-915, DB-181, DB-663, DB-754, DB-908**

33. Stardust, Billion-Year-Old Carbon

This palette is for the lover of substantial, muscular colors. Black of the void; brown and green of the earth; peach and red of flesh and blood—as Joni Mitchell sang "We've got to get ourselves back to the garden." **Delicas: DB-318, DB-734, DB-654, DB-1302, DB-274**

Gemstones and glass beads of the earth palette

Radiant Sun Earrings

Designed and created by Margie Deeb

EASY

> The sophistication of these dazzling fire-polished earrings belies their simplicity. Making a pair is fun, easy, and can take less than two hours. But beware: they are addictive. See if you can make just one pair!

Like the sun's rays breaking through the clouds, fire-polished beads radiate light. Margie Deeb's earrings capture the essence of fire—its light and movement.

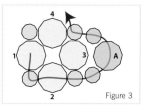

34. Radiant Sun

Inspired by the photo at left, this palette tries to mimic the sun's sheer radiance by using three metallic finishes of gold, a tarnished silver, and copper colors. Accents of the matte gold (DB-331) give the eye a rest and a place to focus. I've omitted the lightest value, opting for the elegance of only metallic colors. If you want to add an ivory for increased contrast, I suggest DB-203. **Delicas: DB-031, DB-254, DB-461, DB-331**

FINISHED LENGTH:
7" TO 7 1/2", DEPENDING
ON CLASP

Materials
- forty 4mm Czech fire-polished metallic rounds, pale gold
- twenty-eight 6mm Czech fire-polished metallic rounds, pale gold
- twenty-eight 8mm Czech fire-polished metallic rounds, pale gold
- fifty-two to fifty-four 11o seed beads, gold
- size D Nymo thread
- size 12 sharp needle
- two earring components: either French ear wires or posts with loop for drops (and 2 jump rings for attaching to posts)

Tools
- pliers for attaching ear wire

Using a 36" piece of Nymo D thread, tie a ring of four 6mm beads together with two overhand knots, leaving a 4" tail (figure 1). Work the tail back into the beads after you've finished each earring.

Pass needle back through bead #1 and bead #2. Add a 4mm bead and pass needle through the 6mm bead #3 as shown in figure 2. (The 4mm is indicated with a more saturated color.) Add a 4mm and pass through each 6mm. Repeat, traveling around the ring until your needle exits the first 4mm strung. Circle through the ring again to secure.

Add one 4mm, one 6mm, and one more 4mm and pass needle through the 4mm bead between bead #3 and bead #4 (figure 3). These 6mm beads are labeled as bead A, bead B, etc.

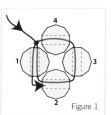

Figure 1

Figure 2

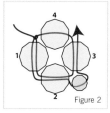

Figure 3

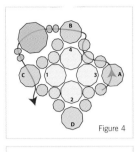

Figure 4

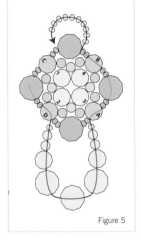

Figure 5

Repeat this step, traveling around the ring until you pass through the first grouping of these three beads. Pass needle through the 4mm between bead #3 and bead #4, and through the 4mm and bead B above them. Add two seed beads, an 8mm bead, and two seed beads. Pass needle through the 6mm bead C (figure 4). Repeat this step, traveling around the ring until you pass through the first grouping of these six beads and have exited 6mm bead D.

Rotate your piece 45 degrees to the right so that the 8mm bead between beads C and B is now the top of the earring. You are ready to add your two loops.

To make the inner loop, add one seed bead, two 4mm beads, one 6mm, three 8mm, one 6mm, two 4mm, one seed bead and insert needle into 6mm bead A. Travel through half the ring as shown in figure 5, exiting the two seed beads to the right of the top 8mm bead.

Add nine or ten seed beads to fit snugly around the top half of the 8mm. Because seed beads differ in width, it may take more or less than ten to fit. Try to use an even number so the same number of seed beads will fall on either side of the earring component when you attach it.

Pass needle through the left half of the earring exiting the 8mm bead between 6mm beads C and D as shown in figure 6, and you are ready to make the outer loop.

String two seed beads, two 4mm, two 6mm, seven 8mm, two 6mm, two 4mm, and two seed beads. Pass through the 8mm and seed beads as shown in figure 6 and then through the rings and both loops several times to secure the entire earring. Knot it with two over-hand knots between beads and clip thread.

Attach the earring component by opening the loop of a French ear wire, or a jump ring, with a pair of pliers. Slip it under the thread wrapped around the top half of the top 8mm bead, between the middle two seed beads at the top of the earring. Close the loop.

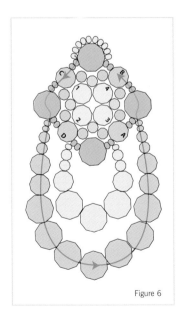

Figure 6

Try these earrings with different-sized loops, bright colors, and color patterns. The one on the left matches the Japanese beetle palette for the Sparkling Draped Loop Collar on page 137.

Lagoon Beaded Belt

Designed and created by SaraBeth Cullinan

EASY

> SaraBeth Cullinan combines jewel tones from the air and water palette to create a sparkling belt of analogous purples, blues, and cool teal green

35. The Lagoon

This combination air-and-water palette is gorgeous and so easy to work with. If you omit the white, any proportions of any of the four colors will combine beautifully. If you include the white, limit it to precisely planned accents. **Delicas:** DB-165, DB-1345, DB-920, DB-215, DB-1490

FINISHED LENGTH: 33" DIAMETER; SWAG IS 13"

Materials
- eight-two 3mm Swarovski crystal bicones, aqua
- seventy-four 3mm Swarovski crystal bicones, capri
- forty-eight 3mm Swarovski crystal rounds, violet opal
- twenty-five 4mm Swarovski crystal bicones, capri
- forty-nine 4mm Swarovski crystal bicones, aqua AB
- twenty-five 2X 4mm Swarovski crystal rounds, capri AB
- seventy-three AB 3mm fire polish rounds, light sapphire
- forty-nine 4mm fire polish rounds, dark sapphire opal
- twenty-four 6mm fire polish rondelles, aqua
- twenty-five 6mm fire polish rounds, fuchsia/amethyst
- forty-eight 6mm fire polish rounds, capri AB
- twenty-four 6mm barrel ovals, cobalt
- twelve 7mm Russian cuts, teal-blue zircon (also called "Blue Zircon Russian Cuts")
- twenty-four7mm Russian cuts, cobalt
- seventy-three 4mm Czech glass rounds, capri opal
- ninety-eight 4mm fresh water pearls, light aqua
- forty-nine 5mm fresh water pearls, purple
- seventy-four 4mm rounds, sterling
- twenty-five 5mm rounds, pewter
- one mermaid hook and eye clasp, pewter
- two 3-hole spacer bars, pewter
- three 3-strand end connectors
- two sea horse charms, pewter
- one whale charm, pewter
- three 4mm jump rings
- twelve crimp tubes
- thirteen feet .014 beading wire

Tools
- wire cutters
- crimping pliers
- chain nose pliers

An abstract photo sparked this project's intensified sea and sky color palette. SaraBeth Cullinan added emerald green and silver to make it her own, rounding out the scheme. Necklace photograpgh by Haigwood Studios

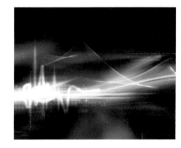

Russian cut glass beads

Attach a 34" piece of wire to the top loop of the 3-strand end connector with a crimp tube. String on one each of:

3mm aqua crystal
4mm capri AB 2X crystal
3mm light sapphire AB fire polish
4mm light aqua pearl
3mm capri crystal
pewter round
4mm capri crystal
6mm fuchsia/amethyst fire polish
sterling round
6mm cobalt barrel oval
sterling round
4mm aqua AB crystal
3mm capri crystal
4mm capri opal glass round
4mm light aqua pearl
3mm aqua crystal
4mm dark sapphire opal fire polish
purple pearl
4mm dark sapphire opal fire polish
3mm aqua crystal
4mm light aqua pearl
3mm light sapphire AB fire polish
4mm capri opal glass round
cobalt Russian cut
4mm capri opal glass round
3mm violet opal crystal
6mm capri AB fire polish
3mm violet opal crystal
4mm light aqua pearl
5mm purple pearl
3mm light sapphire AB fire polish
6mm capri AB fire polish
sterling round
aqua rondelle
3mm capri crystal
4mm aqua AB crystal
Continued, right column

Continued from left column:
teal-blue zircon Russian cut
4mm aqua AB crystal
3mm capri crystal
aqua rondelle
sterling round
6mm capri AB fire polish
3mm light sapphire AB fire polish
purple pearl
aqua pearl
3mm aqua crystal
3mm violet opal crystal
6mm capri AB fire polish
3mm violet opal crystal
4mm capri opal glass round
cobalt Russian cut
4mm capri opal glass round
3mm light sapphire AB fire polish
aqua pearl
3mm aqua crystal
4mm dark sapphire opal fire polish
purple pearl
4mm dark sapphire opal fire polish
3mm aqua crystal
4mm aqua AB crystal
sterling round
6mm cobalt barrel oval
sterling round
6mm fuchsia/amethyst fire polish
4mm capri AB 2X crystal
pewter round
3mm capri crystal
aqua pearl
3mm light sapphire AB fire polish
3mm aqua crystal
3-hole spacer bar

Stringing pattern repeated three times for each strand, on three different strands.

Repeat for a total of three sections. Add on a crimp tube and another 3-strand end connector. Pass back through the tube and crimp. Repeat entire stringing pattern to make two additional strands.

Attach one half of the mermaid clasp to each side of the belt with a 4mm jump rings.

Attach a 12" piece of wire to an outer loop of the 3-strand connector. Repeat the stringing sequence above then add on a crimp tube and the sea horse charm. Pass back through the tube and crimp. Make a second strand for the other outer loop.

Attach a 15" piece of wire to the center loop of the 3-strand connector. Repeat the entire string sequence from above, then reverse from the 4mm capri AB 2X crystal to the purple pearl. Add on a crimp tube and whale charm. Pass back through the tube and crimp closed. Attach to the eye side of the clasp with a 4mm jump ring.

Pewter charms on ends of tassels

Mermaid belt clasp

Mermaid's Collar

Designed and created by Margie Deeb

INTERMEDIATE

Tropical blue-greens fan out in a collar tipped in bubbles of silver and facets of teal. These transparent colors of the oceans offer depth, reflection, and a fluid movement of light. Make sure you are comfortable with basic wire wrapping before beginning this necklace.

Margie Deeb uses radiant bursts of turquoise, teal, and silver to affect the clear, fresh, relaxed palette of tropical waters.

36. Mermaid's Collar

The undersea photo (left) inspired this naturally harmonious, analogous wash of blues and greens. The darker tones are opaque and muted in color. One mid-tone, DB-793, is quite vivid and the lights are highly reflective. **Delicas: DB-788, DB-798, DB-878, DB-793, DB-078, DB-1506**

FINISHED LENGTH: 14"

Materials
- nineteen 1 20-gauge 1/2-hard sterling headpins
- nineteen 3 20-gauge 1/2-hard sterling eye pins
- fourteen 6mm sterling round beads (seamless)
- nineteen 8mm sterling round beads (seamless)
- one 10mm sterling round beads (seamless)
- 18" .019 beading wire
- two .038 3mm sterling crimp beads
- two 3mm sterling crimp covers
- one sterling clasp
- nineteen 8mm Czech fire-polish round faceted beads, teal
- six 6mm Czech fire-polish round faceted beads, teal
- thirty-one 6mm Czech glass cube beads diagonally drilled, aqua
- thirty-four 9mm wide oval or oval faceted beads, teal
- seven 2cm high glass vintage flat beads, pale green
- 2gms size 11o seed beads, aqua luster
- 2gms size 8o seed beads (or #5 triangle beads), silver lined teal iris

Tools
- chain-nose and round-nose pliers
- wire cutters
- crimping tool

To create a faceted bead drop dangle, place an 8mm faceted teal bead onto a headpin. Cut the headpin so it is the length of the bead plus 3/8". Grasp the wire with a round-nose pliers and bend, making a complete circle (figure 1). With the round-nose pliers, close the loop so there is no gap (figure 2).

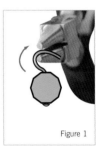

Figure 1

With the chain-nose pliers, open the loop of an eye pin by swiveling the end of the loop to the side (don't pull it straight out, because you won't be able to maintain its shape when closing it). Hook the loop of the bead drop onto the opened eye pin loop. With the round-nose pliers, close the eye pin loop so there is no gap (figure 3.) Make nineteen dangles and attach them to eye pins.

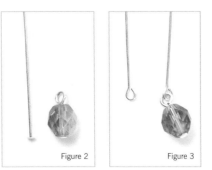

Figure 2

Figure 3

Thread each of the eye pins as shown in figure 4. From the bottom up:

Stack A (make six):
6mm sterling round, 7mm oval, 11o seed, 8mm diagonal cube, 11o seed, 8o seed or triangle bead.

Stack B (make six):
6mm sterling round, 7mm oval, 11o seed, 8mm diagonal cube, 11o seed, 6mm faceted, 8o seed or triangle bead.

Stack C (make six):
7mm sterling round, 7mm oval, 11o seed, 8mm diagonal cube, 11o seed, 2cm vintage flat, 11o seed, 8o seed or triangle bead.

Center Stack D (make one):
10mm sterling round, 7mm oval, 11o seed, 8mm diagonal cube, 8mm diagonal cube, 2cm vintage flat, 11o seed, 8mm diagonal cube, 11o seed, 8o seed or triangle bead.

Stringing Pattern:
Starting from
either side of
center stack D:

one 6mm sterling
one teal oval
Stack C

one 8o
one 7mm sterling
one diagonal cube
Stack C

one 8o
one teal oval
Stack C

one 8o
one 7mm sterling
one diagonal cube
Stack B

one 8o
one teal oval
Stack B

one 8o
one 7mm sterling
one diagonal cube
Stack B

one 8o
one teal oval
Stack A

one 8o
one 7mm sterling
one diagonal cube
Stack A

one 8o
one teal oval
Stack A

one 8o
one 7mm sterling

Crimp bead

A	B	C	Center D
(6)	(6)	(6)	(1)

Figure 4

Figure 5

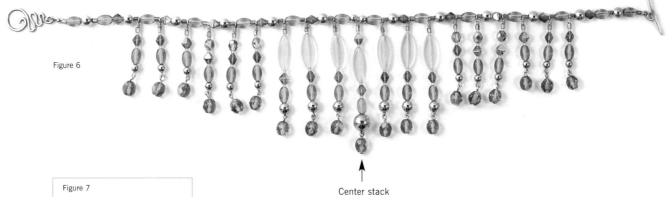

Figure 6

Center stack

Figure 7

Figure 8

Make wrapped loops on each eye pin (figure 5), following the first five steps of the cone instructions on page 171.

Cut an 18" length of beading wire. The left and right sides of the necklace are mirror images of each other, so begin working from the center. Thread the wire through the loop of the tallest stack of beads (D) and work outward to the ends following the stringing pattern (figure 6). The goal is to create enough space between each stack so the stacks are well defined, but not so far apart that the necklace looks sparse.

Crimp the crimp beads (figure 7) as shown on page 170. You could stop now, but why? Concealing the crimp bead with a sterling silver crimp cover finishes the piece beautifully, and looks like another sterling round bead (figure 8).

The cliff face of an open pit copper mine in the southwestern United States illustrates the natural copper and green color pairing that inspired the raku disks and necklace.

FINISHED LENGTH: 32"

Materials
• one 2¼" diameter clay donut pendant, off-center hole
• one 2" diameter clay donut disks, center hole
• one 1⅝" diameter clay donut disks, center hole
• 5gms each 11o seed beads:
  - aqua matte transparent iris (AMTI)
  - gold luster transparent brown (GLTB)
  - opaque aqua (OA)
  - opaque brown (OB)
• twenty-eight 8o seed beads, copper
• size D Nymo thread
• size 12 sharp needle
• vermeil clasp
• hypo cement or clear nail polish

Clay Disk Pendant

Designed and created by Margie Deeb
Raku disks by Michael Stedman

ADVANCED

The color combination of copper and green is a natural one. Copper oxidizes to gorgeous shades of green and blue-green, like those of the Statue of Liberty. Matching seed beads to these shades creates a lively palette that shimmers, even though all the materials are essentially opaque.

37. Inside the Copper Mine

A palette lifted out of the copper mines includes DB-915 with its lined shimmering finish and metallic copper penny (DB-040). Light and deep teal create the oxidized verdigris look. Try red and green aventurine for a similar gemstone palette. **Delicas: DB-915, DB-040, DB-375, DB-788**

On a 34" piece of Nymo D thread, loop through one 11o stop bead that you will remove later. To make the foundation, string two 8o seed beads. Pass needle back up through the first bead, down through the second, and back up through the first bead.

String two more 8o seed beads (#3 and #4). Pass down through #2, up through #1 and #3, down through #4 and #2, and up through #1 and #3 (figure 1).

String 2" of AMTI (figure 2). Loop through the 2" disk. Pass needle down through foundation beads #3 and #1.

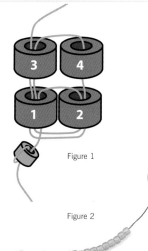

Figure 1

Figure 2

String 1½" AMTI and loop through main pendant. Pass needle up through bead #1 and #3. Pass needle under threads connecting beads #3 and #4 and make small knot (figure 3). Tie a knot onto connecting threads after making each loop. Pass needle down through #4 and #2, and up through #1 and #3 again.

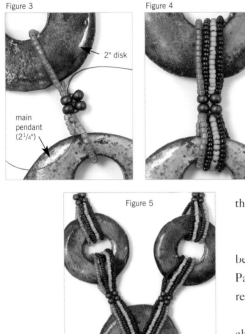

Figure 3

Figure 4

Figure 5

String 2" of GLTB. Loop through the 2" disk. Pass needle down through beads #3 and #1.

String 1½" GLTB and loop through main pendant. Pass needle up through bead #1 and #3. Knot onto connector threads and pass down through beads #4 and #2.

String 1½" OA and loop through main pendant. Pass needle up through beads #2 and #4. Knot onto connector threads.

String 2" OA and loop through 2" disk. Pass needle down through beads #4 and #2. Knot.

String 1½" OB and loop through main pendant. Pass needle up through beads #2 and #4. Knot.

String 2" OB and loop through the 2" disk. Pass down through beads #4 and #2.

Knot thread onto connector threads between beads #1 and #2. Remove stop bead. Tie the working thread and the tail thread together with two overhand knots. Pass threads through as many beads as possible to secure. Clip ends and hide any remaining visible thread within beads (figure 4).

To connect the 2" disk to both 1⅝" disks repeat the above ten steps, however, always string 2 inches of 11o seed beads to make the loops.

To connect the 1⅝" disks to the main strands:

Build two foundations of four 8o beads as in the first two steps above. Make four seed bead loops on these, all exiting the same side of the foundation and looping around each 1⅝" disk (figure 5). Knot onto connecting threads between each loop as before.

With a 36" thread, build another four 8o bead foundation. Remove stop bead and tie the two thread ends together in a double overhand knot. Weave the shorter tail into beads later.

Attach the working thread to the clasp by looping it around the clasp twice and passing needle back through corresponding bead stack of the foundation (figure 6). Pass the needle back down through the foundation where you exited.

String the length of beads you desire (minus length of clasp). I strung 7 inches. Pass needle through corresponding foundation beads that connect to the 1⅝" disk (figure 7). Knot onto connecting threads, pass back up through foundation stack. String next strand the exact same length. Be sure to arrange the colors of the 11o seed beads so they align with the seed bead loops, giving the appearance that they are connected.

When you reach the clasp end again, loop thread through clasp at least twice. Pass back down into foundation and keep stringing. Repeat until you've strung all four strands of 11o seed beads, looping through clasp as much as possible. Tie off, clip, and hide thread within the beads. Repeat for other side of necklace (figure 8).

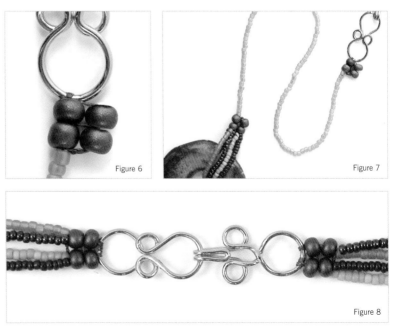

Figure 6

Figure 7

Figure 8

ARTISTS' HISTORICAL PALETTES

Margie Deeb's earrings and broad collar use the classic Egyptian colors of gold, verdigris turquoise, lapis blue, and red glass.

ANCIENT EGYPT

> Because much of their art was religious, the ancient Egyptians used color to symbolically convey messages rather than for realistic portrayal. Minerals and metals were used for their spiritual and therapeutic values. Lapis lazuli, for example, corresponded with joy; turquoise with delight. Some were identified with specific deities—copper and malachite with the goddess Hathor; and gold with the deity of the sun.

The wealth of magnificent jewelry the Egyptians left us employs a wide range of stones including quartz crystal, carnelian, amethyst, jasper, onyx, and lapis along with silver and gold.

Their limited painting palette—the yellow-red of the desert, the blue of the river, the green of papyrus, and the pale blue of the sky—represented the Nile valley landscape.

The ancient Egyptians developed the art of glass, and their glass beads, which held spiritual and magical properties, were the finest of the ancient world.

Bas-relief of winged falcon at Karnak Temple

Two goddesses pray to the scarab as a symbol of the sun god Ra. Pectoral of carnelian faience, circa 12 B.C.

Erich Lessing / Art Resource, NY

38. Color Like an Egyptian

Like many Egyptian artifacts, Tutankhamen's death mask (above) is gold inlaid with gemstones of lapis, carnelian, and turquoise—an instantly recognizable Egyptian palette, rich and bold. **Delicas: DB-031, DB-277, DB-378. DB-793**

39. Winged Falcon at Karnak Temple

Opaque beads colored in soft, dusty tones recall the ancient painted bas-relief of the temple (left) and are perfect for pictorial or exotic applications. A thickly textured multi-strand or patterned woven bracelet, perhaps? **Delicas: DB-353, DB-798, DB-795, DB-651, DB-375**

40. Scarab Pectoral

The Egyptians were masters of glasswork, and simulating precious gemstones out of faience became a specialty. This bold color scheme takes its inspiration from a faience pectoral (left), in which the scarab represents the sun god, Ra. **Delicas: DB-918, DB-238, DB-795, DB-215, DB-301**

41. Throne of the Pharaoh

Black, gold, and ivory—a classic palette also present in Tutankhamen's tomb, where a 28-inch-high ebony chair decorated with ivory inlay and gilded panels was found. Clean lines and a bold arrangement of these highly contrasting tones are perfect for any sophisticated evening adornment. **Delicas: DB-010, DB-203, DB-031**

Colors of the famous dolphin mural
from the Palace of Knossos inspired
Paulette Baron's *Minoan Spirals*.
Glass seed beads, variation of
peyote stitch

Palace of Minos, Knossos, Crete, Greece

ANCIENT MINOA

With their reverence for the Goddess and delight in nature, the
Minoans left the world a legacy of beauty and joy—and it shows in
their colors.

From roughly 3650–1100 B.C., this matriarchal society flourished on Crete. The subjects of their art were images of
nature, court, and religious life. Palace frescoes display vivid Minoan palettes. On one wall we see flourishing animals,
plants, or people; on the opposing walls we are met with an expanse of striking color. Their ceramics were just as
colorful and light-hearted.

Minoans excelled in jewelry and metalwork, reaching mastery in engraving on semi-precious stones such as
agate, hematite, jasper, agate, chalcedony, and rock crystal.

The Minoans would have loved adorning themselves in Jamie Cloud Eakin's embroidered coral and sodalite cabochons. The striking colors form a common Minoan fresco palette.
Coral, sodalite, Brazilian agate, and freshwater pearls

Lilies. Fresco from Akrotiri, Thera (Santorini).

Prince with Lilies. Palace of Minos, Knossos, Crete, Greece

42. Lilies Fresco

This palette began with the colors in the fresco from Akrotiri (left), but quickly took its own course. As if mixing paint, I've combined some colors to arrive at a palette related to that of *Prince of the Lilies*, but is not a direct match. These hues combine to make a soft, quiet color scheme, sophisticated in its use of dulled tones. **Delicas: DB-883, DB-376, DB-622, DB-272, DB-377**

43. Prince of Gigli

Also called *Prince of the Lilies*, this fresco from the Palace of Minos (bottom left) places light buttercup yellow, light warm flesh, and pale sapphire against the strong brick red found in many other frescoes. The smallest amount of black rounds out a palette that is at once gentle and powerful. **Delicas: DB-773, DB-233, DB-208, DB-1475, DB-301**

44. Processional

Similar to the *Prince of Gigli* palette, this scheme is energized by an unusual, contemporary yellow green (DB-687). The yellow has been strengthened, the flesh brightened, and the blue more saturated, so the colors are more playful and stylized, like the processional fresco that inspired it. **Delicas: DB-773, DB-651, DB-1502, DB-240, DB-301, DB-687**

45. The Bull-Jumpers

According to what we glean from frescoes, women and men participated in bull-jumping, which was a sport demanding courage and agility. The famous fresco plays upon the exciting, energetic combination of various blues and oranges. Chalcedony, blue lace agate, yellow-orange tinged jaspers, and carnelian echo this combination beautifully. **Delicas: DB-240, DB-653, DB-277, DB-203, DB-773, DB-310**

Nimatallah / Art Resource, NY

Vanni / Art Resource, NY

EARLY CIVILIZATIONS

Mesopotamia is home to some of the oldest empires in the world. No longer relegated to ritual, body adornment became a way of displaying social status as well. Throughout ancient societies we find the use of red in the form of carnelian and agates, blue in lapis lazuli, and silver and gold. All of these materials were present in the royal tombs of Ur, dating from 2600–2100 B.C.

Herodotus described Babylon as the city of splendor. Brilliant color shimmered from its structures of molded glazed brick. Relief figures in white, black, blue, red, and yellow decorated the city's gates and buildings.

The Etruscans founded European civilization. Theirs was an exuberant and refined culture known now for their granulation-style gold jewelry, exquisite engraved stone jewelry, colorful pottery, and frescoes.

Afghanistan was a center for agate and jasper bead making, and a major supplier of raw materials and beads to surrounding areas.

The Phoenicians, leading navigators and traders, excelled in gem and glass inlaid ivory carvings with gold leaf, as well as three-dimensional glass "sculpture" beads depicting human and animal heads.

Beads of carnelian, a variety of chalcedony, were used throughout the Mesopotamian valley. History inspired Kimberley Price to combine these large faceted stones with silver for a bold design.
Vintage Turkoman focal bead; drop by Tibetan refugees in Nepal

Enameled tiles, mythical animals, lions, and gods embellish the main gate of Babylon, which was dedicated to goddess Ishtar.

Eric Lessing / Art Resource, NY

46. Winged Lions of the Ishtar Gate

Lining the main gate of Babylon are finely detailed lions (left), bulls, and dragons composed in low-relief on ceramic bricks. Imagine how splendid the huge entrance would have looked as you approached—an expanse of rich blue Enameled tile, blue-greens, and warm yellow dotted with white and cream. **Delicas: DB-798, DB-069, DB-729, Db-651, DB-203**

47. Assyrian Splendor

Gold, carnelian, lapis, and malachite were favorite jewelry gemstones of the Assyrians (right). Here I've imitated the palette in glass beads, and used a red that is cooler than most carnelian. I like the flair that a shimmering, crystal-lined red injects into this elegant primary scheme. **Delicas: DB-031, DB-098, DB-726, DB-919**

48. Persian Pottery

Bold, bright, and beautiful, these shapely glass juglets from the 6th century B.C.E. (left) use such contemporary colors they could have been made yesterday. A mixture of matte and reflective beads adds a playful flavor. **Delicas: DB-165, DB-310, DB-233**

Core-made glass juglets, Persian Period. 6th B.CE.

Eric Lessing / Art Resource, NY

Gold, carnelian, lapis lazuli, malachite and imitation rock crystal form this Assyrian necklace dating from the 14th–13th B.C.E.

Bildarchiv Preussischer Kulturbesitz / Art Resource, NY

Funerary chorus of women from a tomb in Ruvo. 5th century B.C.E. Museo Archeologico Nazionale, Naples, Italy

Etruscan banquet fresco. 6th century BCE.

49. Etruscan Funerary Chorus

An inherent sense of harmony graces these near-complementary colors (above). Muted browns and soft, foggy blues speak in restrained tones, while lone accents of red and black, the strongest colors in the group, add vigor, making a robust, unconventional palette. **Delicas: DB-901, DB-361, DB-376, DB-121, DB-781, DB-654, DB-310**

50. Etruscan Banquet Fresco

The stylized fresco from the Tomb of the Lioness accomplishes an extraordinarily rich earth palette (above). Add luminosity by using an AB finish (DB-862), a silver-lined opal finish (DB-1451), and a luster finish (DB-116). **Delicas: DB-116, DB-1451, DB-312, DB-794, DB-373, DB-781, DB-862, DB-310**

51. The Elegance of the Etruscans

Patterns made with fine gold wire (filigree) and minute gold granules characterize Etruscan jewelry. They set contrasting colors of glass paste was among the exquisite detail. 24kt gold and cobalt blue with a luster finish make a timelessly elegant combination. **Delicas: DB-031, DB-277**

52. Metal Arts

The mastery of carving and metalwork of ancient civilizations is astounding. These colors based on bronze metalwork, fine ivory inlay, and copper from the Assyrians create a strong, facile palette. Use for either lavish or simple designs. If you want, substitute silver or black for the charcoal gray. **Delicas: DB-022, DB-203, DB-040, DB-301**

53. Phoenician Glass Elegance

Inspired by Phoenician glass, shades of mauve on a pale cream color with a silver-lined opal finish create a refined combination. **Delicas: DB-1451, DB-629, DB-695, DB-799**

History has seen both jewelry used as currency, and currency used as jewelry. Ilene Combs Blanco combines African coins with lapis, citrine, pewter, and glass beads to create an historical, ethnic look for a pendant necklace.

Stained glass reached its height in the Middle Ages. These rainbows of transparent color inspired Robin Atkins to create this finger-woven beaded tassel.

MEDIEVAL & BYZANTINE

The broad reach of time we call the Middle Ages, or the Medieval period, included major societal upheavals: invasions, explosive population, declining economy and trade, and the plague.

Art historians classify Medieval art into major periods and movements. In addition, each "nation" or culture in the Middle Ages had its own distinct style. Medieval art included many crafts, such as mosaics, calligraphy, illuminated manuscripts, textiles, tapestries, woodwork, and sculpture.

Byzantine art is the glory of the Middle Ages. The capitol of the Byzantine Empire was the city of Constantinople, known today as Istanbul. From about the fifth century until 1453, the purpose of its art was the glorification of God and Jesus. State sanctioned Christianity created a new style in the visual arts as the Christian story, its heralds, and its icons became central to all images.

Shimmering mosaics and the painting of icons became original art forms. Depiction of space and perspective was replaced with extraordinary use of surface decoration and color. Glittering, multi-hued fragments of tile and glass displayed wealth and provided a spiritual atmosphere of transcendent light.

Byzantine jewelry employed all sorts of colored stones in cloisonné, cabochon, and bead form: emeralds, sapphires, topaz, aquamarines, rubies, garnets, amethysts, and pearls.

Jean Campbell's peyote-stitched *Star of India* brings to mind the exquisite goldsmithing and rich palettes of Byzantium. Swarovski crystals, and glass beads; sculptural peyote stitch and fringe variation

Laborers Build Fortress from the Bayeux Tapestry circa 1066

Coronation Order. Ca. 1330

54. Bayeux Tapestry

Elegant in their mellowed restraint, the embroidered Bayeaux Tapestries depicting the battle of 1066 (left), inspired this palette. I took liberties with the tones and added a green. Five matte finishes make up this low-key, low-intensity, and low-contrast scheme. **Delicas: DB-388, DB-773, DB-781, DB-311, DB-377**

55. Coronation Order

Warm tones from an illuminated manuscript (left) inspired these soft hues. The first three shades are light and airy, elevating the overall tone. These alone make a beautiful shell-inspired trio. Add a muted blue and matte metallic soft green, and you've got an unconventional, sophisticated palette. **Delicas: DB-1478, DB-1459, DB-1302, DB-361, DB-373**

56. Lady and the Unicorn

Medieval tapestries are some of the most beautiful in existence. In many of them we find exquisite details woven against a rich red background. Here I've used a gold luster transparent dark red as a foundation, and added a silver-lined opal finish that is a creamy off-white rather than white (DB-1451). Finish is the key to this palette's luxury. **Delicas: DB-105, DB-1451, DB-181, DB-183, DB-689**

57. Vienna Genesis

The silver lettering on a rich, purple background of the Vienna Genesis codex inspired this luxurious combination. Try different shades of purples. The DB-922 suggested here is lined in blue, and offers its blue cast. Any shade of amethyst harmonizes beautifully with silver (actually a white gold in DB-032). **Delicas: DB-922, DB-032**

Byzantine Mosaic,
Hagia Sophia

Adoration of the Magi
Lorenzo Monaco, 1422

58. Virgin and Child of Hagia Sophia

A mosaic inside the Hagia Sophia in Istanbul (above) uses dulled blues and pale flesh colors accented with muted green, red, and white to depict the mother and child. A variety of gold tesserae form a sparkling background for the restrained robes. I've prescribed three shades of gold to achieve that effect. **Delicas: DB-031, DB-331, DB-621, DB-377, DB-208, DB-817, DB-654, DB-203**

59. Adoration of the Magi

Lorenzo Monaco, painter and Camaldolite monk, used an extraordinarily bright range of colors for his time. The central panel of this altar triptych (above) is dominated by golds reds, and oranges, making the piece glow with warmth. I've cut back on the amount of colors, but have not sacrificed luster. Copper accents add depth. **Delicas: DB-031, DB-683, DB-161, DB-182, DB-461**

60. Constantine's Delight

The emperor would have paid well for anything in this palette. Five silver-lined and matte silver-lined jewel tones form a pure, saturated palette. Surround them with 24kt gold (DB-031) for a sumptuous effect. As a counterpoint to that highly reflective gold, accent with 24kt matte finish (DB-331). **Delicas: DB-031, DB-161, DB-696, DB-683, DB-605, DB-610, DB-331**

61. Roman Mosaics

Romans preferred opaque marble tesserae rather than transparent sparkling glass. This palette imitates the less effusive Roman mosaics by using mostly opaque colors with matte finished gold. Use red and black only as accents so they don't overwhelm. **Delicas: DB-331, DB-919, DB-277, DB-203, DB-654, DB-310**

Like a Byzantine mosaic, splinters of color radiate from Marcia Decoster's *Terracita* necklace.
Glass seed beads and cut-glass crystal

THE RENAISSANCE

During the fourteenth through sixteenth centuries, beginning in Florence and spreading elsewhere, artists turned to the direct study of nature for accurate visual representation. They also turned back to the classical art of ancient Greek and Roman history and mythology for inspiration and subject matter. They wanted to endow art with beauty and significance far beyond that found in nature. In essence, they sought to transcend nature through art.

No longer regarded as an artisan, for the first time in written history the artist emerged as an independent personality. The height of this period brought us the creative genius of Leonardo DaVinci, Michelangelo, and Raphael. These masters used color in service of unity, harmony, and balance.

In Venice, color and its careful application was deemed fundamental to the life-force of a painting. Over time, however, Venetian artists gradually softened their colors to more accurately portray nature. In Florence color was often more vivid.

Because fabric hues evolved from organic dyes, colors were softer than those we wear today. Some of the more unusual names given to fashionable colors were Horseflesh, The Devil in the Head, Kiss-Me-Darling, Ape's Laugh, and Scratch Face. We can only guess what shade some of these bizarre names represented.

Neutral mineral colors from a slice of the Sistine Chapel influenced Jamie Cloud Eakin's palette.
Agate, petrified wood, yellow calcite, freshwater pearls, Picasso jasper, gold coral, dendritic opal, and rhodonite cabochons and beads

Madonna and Child
Giovanni Bellini (1430–1516)

62. Bellini's *Madonna and Child*

Pale blue reveals the rigorous nature of a transparent luster red, and the contrast between the two, while unexpected, is oddly pleasing. As companion shades, cream (DB-1451) and an AB finished flesh (DB-069) balance the high contrast. Accents of rich matte brown (DB-312) amplify the effect of the red.
Delicas: DB-218, DB-116, DB-1451, DB-069, DB-312

Portrait of a Lady with an Ermine
Leonardo DaVinci, Ca. 1490.

Young Girl with a Book by
Bronzino, 1545. Uffizi.
Florence, Italy

63. *Portrait of a Lady with an Ermine*

In *Portrait of a Lady with an Ermine*, (above) DaVinci relies on the contrasts of dark umbers against light, warm flesh colors to set a stately mood. To make this palette sing, punctuate these main colors with muted, primary accents and create an arresting focal point with red. **Delicas: DB-769, DB-764, DB-353, DB-742, DB-377, DB-654**

64. Titian the Venetian

A supreme colorist, Titian is among the greatest painters of the Western world. This palette is inspired by the force of his painting, *Venus of Urbino* in which deep Venetian reds are featured against warm ivory-gold flesh and pale, neutral linen-whites. **Delicas: DB-280, DB-378, DB-654, DB-353, DB-1500**

65. Beautiful Bellini

Bellini revolutionized Venetian painting, moving it towards a more sensuous and coloristic style with his deep, rich tints and detailed shadings This sumptuous combination of gold, blue, and yellow could have been lifted from one of his paintings. **Delicas: DB-031, DB-707, DB-920, DB-233**

66. Bronzino Blue

A classic blue and brown combination, like Bronzino's portrait (above right), is augmented in beads by replacing brown with a deep copper metallic color, and adding an AB finish. Cream accents (DB-203) add contrasting high notes. A palette of refined grace and style. **Delicas: DB-377, DB-461, DB-069, DB-203**

67. Raphael's *Lambent Light*

This eight-color palette is easy to work with because all the tones are so closely related. From the sumptuous surface detail of Raphael's *Portrait of a Woman* (bottom left) these warm, substantial, golden-tinged hues get a boost in beads by two AB finishes. The delicacy of the amber, beige, and cream are well grounded in a foundation of deep umber (DB-312), the force of the whole scheme. **Delicas: DB-312, DB-764, DB-101, DB-054, DB-205, DB-031, DB-883, DB-068**

68. Bacchiacca Tapestry

A palette of rich deep reds, softened muted yellows, and chestnut browns decorate the elaborate Renaissance tapestries designed by painter Francesca Ubertini. Use only the smallest tingling accents of blue to contrast the warmth. **Delicas: DB-031, DB-233, DB-654, DB-1451, DB-764, DB-285**

69. Portrait of Elisabeth of Valois

The first successful female painter of the Renaissance, Sofonisba Anguissola painted vibrant portraits for the Spanish court. Black and browns dominate, while jewels and intricate embroidery shimmer in red, gold, and ivory. **Delicas: DB-287, DB-310, DB-654, DB-204, DB-031**

Woman, an embroidered pendant by Frieda Bates, conveys the dignified, harmonious Renaissance palette of muted tones from Raphael's *Madonna of the Goldfinch*.
Glass beads, shell

Madonna of the Goldfinch by Raphael. Uffizi. Florence, Italy

Portrait of a Woman
Raphael, 1515

BAROQUE

Following the age of discovery that marked the Renaissance, the Baroque age of expansion encompasses seventeenth- and early eighteenth-century European art. As its art spread outward from Rome, each country added its influence to come up with a Baroque style of its own. The various styles became complex and contradictory, but underlying them all are drama, vitality, movement, tension, and emotional exuberance. In general, the goal of Baroque art was to evoke emotion by appealing to the senses in dramatic ways. Much of the Italian Baroque tended toward overwhelmingly grandiose displays, like Bernini's opulent and extravagant chapel and adornments of St. Peter's Basilica.

Spirit Dancer
Frieda Bates' gold and dichroic glass necklace takes its sensual richness from Baroque interiors.

Baroque painters were fascinated with light, be it in sharp and sudden bursts, or slightly shifting modulations. The intense drama of Caravaggio's paintings come from his sharply defined light with deep obscuring shadows. Rembrandt's work relies on dramatic golden light to portray spiritual stillness.

Vermeer, a poet of light and hue, rendered color amazingly true to life, filling dark shadows with color, and modifying reflective shades.

70. Baroque Grandeur

A sensuous palette of ivory, gold, and marble grayed-pinks mirror the grandeur of the Baroque. The architectural elements of Herrenchiemsee palace hall (left) share warmer versions of these colors, and its palette of ceiling murals includes myriad pastel and muted tones.
Delicas: DB-203, DB-253, DB-728, DB-210, DB-031

71. Heavenly Opulence

Baroque architecture expressed passion and drama through opulence. As you ascend into light at the top of the Herrenchiemsee stairway (left), you are surrounded by theatrical color, sculpture, detail, and movement. **Delicas: DB-773, DB-106, DB-730, DB-257, DB-203, DB-031**

Herrenchiemsee Palace Hall
Bavaria, Germany

Using the gold and black of many a Baroque painting, Margie Deeb creates drama in this necklace of handmade ceramic beads and glass.

Head of a Girl. (Girl with the Pearl Earring)
Vermeer (van Delft), Jan (1632–1675)

Scala / Art Resource, NY

Image licensed from PicturesNow.com

Judith and Her Maidservant
Artemisia Gentileschi, 1620

Image licensed from PicturesNow.com

The Prophet Jeremiah Mourning the Destruction of Jerusalem
Rembrandt, Harmensz van Rijn,1630

ARTISTS' HISTORICAL PALETTES

72. *Girl with a Pearl Earring*

Dutch master painter Johannes Vermeer rendered the effects of light with a precision more subtle and less dramatic than many Baroque artists. In his most famous painting (above), complementary colors, make the image appear to shimmer. The paint has degraded over the centuries, causing, the background to appear black rather than deep transparent green, as Vermeer originally painted it. **Delicas: DB-310, DB-285, DB-730, DB-053, DB-781, DB-353, DB-883**

73. Baldacchino

Bernini, one of the most imaginative and brilliant artists of the Baroque, is considered its most characteristic and sustaining spirit. This combination of metallics and black is inspired by Bernini's baldacchino for St.Peter's Basilica, constructed of extravagantly detailed gilt bronze.
Delicas: DB-310, DB-011, DB-022, DB-254, DB-031

75. Artemisia's Angel

At a time when historic and religious themes were considered beyond a woman's reach, Artemisia Gentileschi was the first female painter to become a member of the Accademia dell' Arte del Disegno in Florence. Her palettes were consistent with the Baroque in heavy darks and stark highlights. This gentler combination represents her ethereal angel panel in the Casa Buonarroti Galleria which uses a simple, sublime harmony based on muted blue and honey tones. **Delicas: DB-285, DB-1537, DB-101, DB-621, DB-278, DB-203**

76. The Richness of Rembrandt

Rather than reproduce Rembrandt's colors, I've tried to simulate the shimmering quality of light (bottom left) his paintings effuse. The warm golden and copper tones are similar in value and share highly reflective surface finishes, creating a gentle, understated palette that glows.
Delicas: DB-461, DB-621, DB-022, DB-101

77. Baroque Drama

The stark contrasts of matte black, galvanized copper, and 24kt gold delivers high drama worthy of a Baroque painting. Bold, simple, and powerful. **Delicas: DB-310, DB-461, DB-031**

The Death of the Virgin
Caravaggio, 1600

74. Caravaggio's Drama

The most influential painter of the Baroque, Caravaggio took the depiction of light and shadow to new levels with his revolutionary technique of tenebrism: dramatic illumination of selected forms from out of dark shadow. This high contrast palette of limited hue honors his contribution to art.
Delicas: DB-734, DB-011, DB-280, DB-654, DB-1302, DB-353

Jamie Cloud Eakin's high-contrast palette of earth tones would have honored Caravaggio, who dismissed the formal colors of the Renaissance for a more realistic, down-to-earth palette. Artist paintbrush jasper cabochon, carved tigereye frog, leopardskin jasper, tigereye, petrified wood, and African mud beads

Room with mirrors
Francois de Cuvillies (1695–1768).
Falkenlust Castle, Bruehl, Germany

Erich Lessing / Art Resource, NY

ROCOCO

Jean Campbell takes the Rococo
approach in her *Bling* bracelet,
going over-the-top. A typical Rococo
interior involved an abundance of
gold and mirrors.
Sleeping Beauty turquoise, vermeil,
gold-plated chain, 14kt gold-plated
and glass beads; tubular peyote stitch

In reaction to the imperious attitude and grandiose formality
of Louis XIV's seventy-two year reign, France focused on more
personal and pleasurable pursuits. Political life and private
morals relaxed, and a new style in art was born: the Rococo.
The word literally means "pebble," and refers to the small
stones and shells used to decorate the interiors of grottoes.

Asymmetrical forms of shell and plant motifs were the visual themes that matched the social air of frivolity, erotic play, and artifice. The Rococo style is primarily one of interiors, surface decoration, and small art. Utensils, furniture, accessories, and objects of all sorts are embellished in a profusion of curving tendrils, sprays of foliage, and shell forms. Salons abound with gilded moldings and daintily colored flowers and garlands.

Porcelain replaced the art of sculpture, and factories hired the most talented French artists to draw and design for their painters. Firing and enameling techniques advanced enabling artists to add rich, deep colors to their pastel palettes.

Like the sumptuous brocades and silks worn in boudoirs, salons, and theaters, Rococo color was both light and cheerful, luxurious and sensual. Boucher's paintings of Madame de Pompadour, Tiepolo's frescoes, and Watteau's delicate shimmering palettes exemplify Rococo color.

Marcia DeCoster loosely based the palette of *Victoria* on that of the Petite Singerie (Little Monkey Room, below) at Château de Chantilly, using a dominant cream color with gold and pastels accents. Yes, there are monkeys to be found in those Rococo murals.

Petite Singerie at Château de Chantilly
Huet, Christophe (d.1759). Musée Condé, Chantilly, France

81. Petite Singerie

A scheme of cream and gold, the mainstay of Rococo palettes, from the Little Monkey Room (left) only this time with less emphasis on pink, and more on other hues as accents. **Delicas: DB-203, DB-031, DB-800, DB-862, DB-691**

Sèvres French vase, 1758

Chinese Teahouse at Sanssouci Palace

Sanssouci Palace
G.W. von Knobelsdorff, 1754–1756.
Sanssouci Palace, Potsdam, Germany

Jean Campbell creates a floral theme in soft pastels to illustrate a delicate Rococo palette.
Rose quartz, ceramic, and glass beads

78. French Vase

The Sèvres vase (left) was the starting point for this slightly cooler, lighter color scheme. DB-621 is a soft gold color with a silver-lined alabaster finish, less brilliant than the gilt ornamentation of the vase. To make this work, make a foundation of the blue and bisque white, using the other four colors as accents. **Delicas: DB-881, DB-1530, DB-621, DB-108, DB-917, DB-281**

79. Lagrenée

Inspired by a Rococo porcelain place setting, I found this combination disconcerting at first. But as I experimented with various hues and surface finishes, I came to like this quirky palette for its unpredictability. The porcelain design by Jean Jacques Lagrenée for Sèvres is an illustration in which crisp, linear, black patterns repeat over a field of pink with one bright area of yellow. Be extra careful with proportions. **Delicas: DB-1457, DB-310, DB-902, DB-053, DB-1483**

80. Weis Church Fresco

Weis church in Bavaria has been called "the perfect church of the German Baroque." Its ceiling depicts the pastel heavens in undulating curves festooned with garlands. Sky blue and cream form the foundation gold and stronger accents. Here I focus on only the blue and pink accents for a delicate Rococo concoction. **Delicas: DB-215, DB-1530, DB-031, DB-920, DB-914**

82. Chinese Teahouse

Pull out the beads to get the full effect of this gorgeous palette. It works even better in beads than on the exterior of the teahouse (left). Pinkish-coral (DB-1523) is perfect in small accents for three shades of a complex, gently muted green and 24kt gold, which sparks the scheme to life. **Delicas: DB-1454, DB-917, DB-1414, DB-031, DB-1523**

83. Sanssouci

Using pale green (DB-1526) as the dominant color works better for me than yellow or bronze, as seen in the exterior of Sanssouci Palace (left). "Sanssouci" means "without care." A playful, care-free palette indeed, yet it took tremendous care to make the proportions and hues work. Add 24kt gold if you want more contrast than the bronze (DB-022) delivers. **Delicas: DB-1526, DB-022, DB-160, DB-217, DB-352**

84. L'Odalisque

I've lifted these powdery soft hues from the canvases of Francois Boucher, who was known for his playful, erotic nudes. His archly posed women lounging about on piles of blue-grey velvet pillows casting inviting smiles represent the Rococo at its height. **Delicas: DB-798, DB-376, DB-353, DB-1302, DB-1451, DB-731**

Morning on the Seine, near Giverny
Claude Monet (1840–1926)

Image licensed from PicturesNow.com

MODERN ART

From the late nineteenth century on, artists rebelled, experimenting with new materials and new ways of seeing. The results examined and redefined the very function of art. We refer to "modern art" as the time when artists parted from representational art.

Movements came and went, centralized in various parts of Europe and America, many overlapping and blending. Each movement had its own ideas about color, its function, and how to use it.

Claude Monet and the Impressionists were obsessed with painting light and used lots of shimmering colors, side by side to achieve fleeting visual sensations.

Post-impressionists expanded upon the Impressionist ways, and developed their own singular style. Van Gogh and Seurat were fascinated with the act of painting itself, focusing on thick swabs of paint or many tiny dots of color. Like a scientist, Cezanne studied and tested color repeatedly to learn what he could of its power to give structure to form. Through color intensity alone, rather than light and dark, he achieved solidity and fullness of form. Gauguin began to free color from its constraints of copying nature, and used brilliant, unpredictable tones and combinations.

The Fauves, (a title which translates as "wild beasts") were the first to unleash color from its traditional role and use it expressively as an end in itself. They distorted subjects and painted them in shockingly brilliant, clashing colors. Henri Matisse never tired of inventing thrilling color combinations.

In Sea to Sky, Robin Atkins reflects Monet's shimmering Impressionist palette.
Vintage Thai silver, pressed glass, and lampworked beads

Composition, 1915
by Wassily Kandinsky (1866–1944)

rich Lessing / Art Resource, NY

Robin Atkins found inspiration for
All That Jazz in the profusion of
color, line, and form of Wassily
Kandinsky's abstract compositions.
Improvisational bead embroidery;
antique pressed glass, blown
glass dangles

Industrial colored dark browns, grays, and greens dominated the
Constructivist palettes. Born in Russia, this experimental, totally abstracted
movement pared images down to their basic geometric elements.

Picasso and Braque founded the intellectual Cubist movement, in which all
kinds of color palettes were used to paint objects as the mind perceives them,
fragmented into several different points of view simultaneously.

Freedom of individual expression was paramount to the Abstract
Expressionists such as Franz Kline, Willem de Kooning, Mark Rothko, Robert
Motherwell, and Jackson Pollock. Some of them rejected color, some used it
sparingly. Some focused on broad fields of tone to convey emotion, others
dripped and splashed it all over huge canvases. For them, color was all about
the glorification of expression and the act of painting.

Andy Warhol blew the lid off color in the Pop Art movement, using garish
combinations. Lichtenstein parodied earlier Modernist styles and made use of
primary palettes in his signature comic-strip frame paintings.

Today, in contemporary art, every color combination and palette can be
found. Some galleries specialize in colorless, monochromatic brown paintings,
while others explode with neon palettes.

The Sower with Setting Sun
Vincent Van Gogh (1853–1890)

Image licensed from Wood River Gallery

85. Van Gogh Warmth

To simplify working with so many colors, think in terms of groups: the warm yellow-oranges and
the lavenders. Yellow-green (DB-372) stands alone as a luscious accent to be used judiciously
and positioned carefully where emphasis is needed. **Delicas: DB-651, DB-773, DB-781, DB-694,
DB-799, DB-372, DB-160, DB-795**

86. Degas' Dancers

This gorgeous variation was inspired by the blue/orange complementary harmony of a Degas pastel
drawing. All is gentle, soft, and muted except a minute and powerfully sharp accent of deep brown
(DB-734). **Delicas: DB-203, DB-208, DB-054, DB-067, DB-788, DB-792, DB-375, DB-734**

87. The Fruit of Cézanne

Cézanne's study of color in nature lasted a lifetime and we reap the benefits. Treat this palette,
taken from the fruit of one of his paintings, as a dominant group of warm yellows with secondary
greens and small accents of pure orange (DB-703). **Delicas: DB-1302, DB-651, DB-233,
DB-272, DB-011, DB-124, DB-687, DB-703**

Franz Marc's vivid palettes create dreamlike worlds where animals live in harmony. Inspired by the *Blue Fillies* Thom Atkins uses these colors to create his own dreamlike landscape of fabric and beads in *Reflections*.
Glass beads on Ultrasuede
Photograph by Haigwood Studios

Blue Fillies
Franz Marc (1880–1916)

Erich Lessing / Art Resource, NY

Piti Teina (*Two Sisters*), 1892
Paul Gauguin (1848–1903)

Image licensed from Wood River Gallery

88. *The Man with the Red Scarf*: Aristide Bruant

Toulouse-Lautrec broke color bounds with his glaring depictions of the tawdry night world of Paris. Inspired by his famous poster, this simple, arresting scheme startles with its bold primaries and the unique inclusion of an odd, almost neutral, bone color (DB-388). **Delicas: DB-310, DB-651, DB-707, DB-388, DB-727**

89. Tropical Brights

Gauguin's rebellious nature and love of brilliant color freed him from the Impressionist palettes of low contrast. He introduced colors from Oceania to modern art. I've omitted the black and flesh tones used in the painting (bottom left) to focus on an array of brights. Use only a speck of blue, as he did for the girl's collar. **Delicas: DB-914, DB-744, DB-160, DB-232, DB-746, DB-919, DB-057**

90. Art Nouveau

Heavily influenced by Japanese prints and exotic styles, the Art Nouveau movement protested against industrialization. This luscious palette is taken from an early 1900s French Art Nouveau cast-gold belt buckle depicting a pair of herons. Blue, green and turquoise colored enamels define their wings. **Delicas: DB-031, DB-793, DB-746, DB-215, DB-1506**

91. Art Deco

Bold, primary colors and black and white dominate the simple lines and geometric shapes of the Art Deco style of the 1920s and 30s. This odd palette comes from an Austrian brooch of stamped and enameled silver. Marcasite is represented by silver-colored white gold (DB-038). **Delicas: DB-310, DB-745, DB-169, DB-233, DB-038**

Mod Squad.
Bright neon colors, like lime green,
became popular in the 1960s.
Lampworked bead by Kristy Nijenkamp
Necklace by Margie Deeb

Pattern designed for wallpaper
and/or fabric
Morris, William (1834–1896))

92. Ships

The first artist recruited to teach at the Bauhaus school was the American painter Lyonel Feininger. Warm greens and yellow dominate the palette from his painting Ships. The smallest tingling accent of blue rivets your focus with its contrasting cool temperature. **Delicas: DB-237, DB-1453, DB-266, DB-776, DB-310, DB-764, DB-285**

93. William Morris

Followers of the Arts and Crafts movement rejected the opulence of the Victorian era, choosing to be inspired by nature and medieval tapestries as they sought to return to a more natural, simple life. Their muted colors often derived from vegetable dyes. This sophisticated combination from a wallpaper design (left) creates an elegant harmony representative of the movement, modern in its own, distinct way. **Delicas: DB-243, DB-257, DB-099, DB-773, DB-731, DB-1452**

94. *From the Lake I*

In this palette representative of Georgia O'Keeffe's sensuous abstracts, a swirl of cool blues and grays are sculpted by accents of maroon and lime green. The body of her work shows the journey to mastery of strong, rich, evocative color. **Delicas: DB-285, DB-881, DB-381, DB-310, DB-200, DB-281, DB-169**

95. Three Musicians

Picasso laid the basis for Cubism, which attempted to represent a simultaneity of viewpoints on a single canvas. Cubist palettes varied greatly, and this is one of the boldest. DB-287 is an AB finish, adding hints of delicate colors Picasso did not include. **Delicas: DB-287, DB-310, DB-200, DB-285, DB-743, DB-745**

96. The Pink Tablecloth

Georges Braque, along with Picasso, established the Cubist still life tradition. In this palette, the soft grays and pale pink (DB-1452) complement the much stronger blue-greens and marigolds. **Delicas: DB-1452, DB-301, DB-731, DB-357, DB-217, DB-651, DB-764**

Cheerful Art Deco pastels decorate
Joan Babcock's *Moroccan Bazaar*.
Cavandoli knotting, wrapping

Art Deco towers on the gateway of
Luna Park in Sydney

Portrait of Adele Bloch-Bauer I
Oil & gold on canvas
Gustav Klimt (1862-1918)

Image licensed from PicturesNow.com

©iStockphoto.com / Mary Johnson

SoBe style in South Beach, Miami, Florida

97. Golden Gustav

The goal of the Symbolists was to see through material things to a significance deeper than the superficial. In search of new form in painting, Gustav Klimt drew inspiration from Byzantine mosaics, embellishing his paintings with gold, silver, and brightly colored tessellated patterns (left). **Delicas: DB-031, DB-203, DB-031, DB-310, DB-295, DB-274, DB-707**

98. Effervescence

Colors explode in jolting contrast and chaos in Hans Hofmann's mixed media painting. This unusual palette calls for just the right kind of vehicle: something casual that makes a bold statement. For a variation, try using black as the dominant color. **Delicas: DB-233, DB-310, DB-914, DB-200, DB-757, DB-919, DB-1495**

99. Marilyn

In the four months following Marilyn Monroe's death, Andy Warhol made more than twenty silkscreen paintings of the star, using brilliant, artificial, non-representational colors. This peculiar combination represents one of the palettes from the series that has become an icon of modern art. **Delicas: DB-244, DB-1526, DB-310, DB-751, DB-757**

100. SoBe Style

Art Deco architecture from the 1930s gives us buildings painted in a colorful array of pastels, like the one shown on the left. Palettes like this are easy to work with. Large playful baubles would work great, especially plastic ones! **Delicas: DB-233, DB-235, DB-917, DB-200**

Ceramic Pendant

Designed and created by Margie Deeb

EASY

Playful, delicate colors in lacquer-like ceramic says "Rococo," as does the curving gold surface decoration. Any pendant can be dropped from the decorative connector ring in the center. Try variations by stacking smaller focal beads on several headpins and draping them from the ring.

Margie Deeb uses the playful colors from Madame de Pompadour's ship-shaped pot-pourri vessel to fashion a pendant necklace of hand-made ceramic beads by Some Enchanted Beading.
In addition to strides made in porcelain production and artistry, the Rococo is also known for the popular "Chinoiserie" style, which attempted to copy Chinese themes in decoration. The vessel below, with its oriental ornamentation, is an example of the eighteenth century fascination with Chinese style.

101. Madame Pompadour

The dominant pink, DB-244, is a perfect Rococo pink: light, festive, and feminine. Teal green, alabaster gold, and ivory comprise the secondary colors. For more depth I've included one of the accent colors from the scene painted on the center front of the vessel in this palette—a cobalt blue with an AB finish (DB-165). **Delicas: DB-244, DB-919, DB-621, DB-203, DB-165**

Joseph-Siffred Duplessis Potpourri "vaisseau" (vessel). Around 1760; Paris, sleeping room of Madame de Pompadour, hotel d'Evreux Sevres semi-porcelain. Louvre, Paris, France

Erich Lessing / Art Resource, NY

FINISHED LENGTH: 10½"

Materials
- ten handmade ceramic beads
- twenty-seven 6mm faceted spacers, rose pink
- eighteen 8mm cube beads, rose alabaster
- twelve 8mm faceted saucer beads, light rose
- .014 beading wire, such as Softflex or Beadalon, gold color (comes packaged in standard length)
- four gold-filled or vermeil crimp beads, .044 ID, 2mm
- decorative gold or vermeil connector ring, 13mm
- gold-filled headpin, 3" or longer
- two 8mm round or twist wire jump rings, gold or vermeil
- two gold-plated seed beads
- clasp, gold or vermeil

Tools
- chain-nose pliers
- crimping tool
- wire cutters

Necklace

Using wire cutters, cut two 11"-long strands of beading wire. Pass one of the wire strands through a gold-plated seed bead and a crimp bead. Run it through one of the rings of the clasp and back through the crimp and seed bead, leaving about a ¾" tail (figure 1). Close the crimp bead as shown on page 170. Do the same with the other beading wire.

String beads onto each wire in the pattern shown in figure 2. Slide beads over the wire tail exiting the seed bead so the tail is concealed. When all beads are on each wire, add a crimp bead to each ends.

Open each jump ring and attach it securely to the decorative connector ring. Close each jump ring tightly so there is no space between the cut ends of the ring.

Run each of the loose ends of the strung beading wire around a jump ring and back through the crimp bead. Pass it through a few more beads that are already on the wire. Using chain nose pliers, gently pull the beading wire tight enough to close any gaps between beads, but not so tight that the beads bunch together. The strands should drape gently.

Closure should look like figure 3.

Pendant

On the headpin, stack beads as shown in figure 3. Finish the headpin as shown on pages 132–133. Attach it to the decorative connector ring while the loop is still open (figure 4). This step must be carried out as precisely as possible. You'll need the wrapping of the headpin to touch the top beads so they don't slide about on the headpin. The wire wrapping must be as neat as possible because it holds the centerpiece of the necklace.

The chalcedony and amazonite necklace on page 24 uses this same technique without a decorative connector ring.

Figure 1

Figure 3

Figure 4

Figure 2

Constructivist Bracelet

Woven by Frieda Bates; Designed by Margie Deeb

INTERMEDIATE

Constructivism grew out of Cubism and Futurism in the 1900s. Committed to total abstraction, Constructivist art pares down reality to basic geometric forms and linear elements, with minimal, simple color palettes.

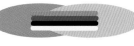

102. The Colors of Constructivism

Neutrals accented by one color, in this case deep teals, were a mainstay of the constructivist palette, though brighter hues were often employed. A few sparkling finishes among matte opaques liven the palette up a bit, despite its moody overtones. **Delicas: DB-761, DB-1456, DB-792, DB-919, DB-310, DB-203**

The design is composed of carefully sized and placed rectangles. Its foreground and background are defined and unified by a sweeping arch.

The bracelet's achromatic, almost industrial color scheme and constructivist design pays homage to the tradition of artists such as Kasimir Malevich, Alexander Rodchenko, and El Lissitzky.

A Constructivist palette–grey, black, white, and metallics– follows the Constructivist tradition of geometric forms.
Design by Margie Deeb
Loomwork by Frieda Bates

Erich Lessing / Art Resource, NY

Life in the Grand Hotel
Malevich, Kazimir (1878–1935)
1913–14

PEYOTE:
   28 BEADS WIDE (1 1/2")
   120 BEADS HIGH (6")*

LOOM:
   28 BEADS WIDE (1 1/2")
   120 BEADS HIGH (6")*

* Measurement does not include length of clasp and findings

Quantity of Beads		Delica Color #	
1 gram	Matte Cream	#352	♥
1 gram	Matte Eggshell	#762	✳
25 beads	Pale Silver Gray	#271	
6 grams	Gargoyle Gray	#301	
1 gram	Tarnished Silver (galvanized)	#254	
40 beads	Ash Gray	#761	
3 1/2 grams	Gunmetal Grey	#001	⬤
2 1/2 grams	Opaque Black	#010	

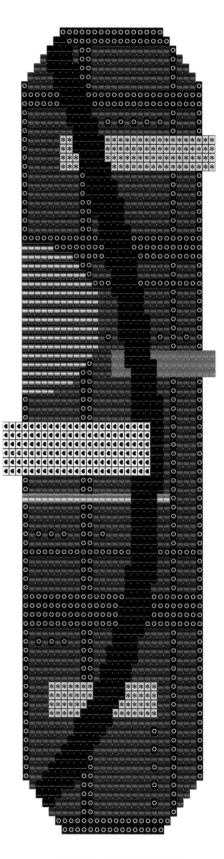

PEYOTE OR BRICK STITCH   LOOM OR SQUARE STITCH

Draped Troy Multi-Strand Necklace

Designed and created by Margie Deeb

ADVANCED

Gold is the solitary member of many a historical jewelry palette. The inspiration for this project—a 4,300-year-old necklace unearthed in the archeological digs of Troy—derives its sumptuous elegance from many textures wrought in gold-plated silver. My updated version uses iridescent topaz-colored glass and vermeil.

Margie Deeb uses glass and vermeil to fashion a grand broad collar inspired by this gilt silver one from 2300 B.C.E. discovered in Troy.

Bildarchiv Preussischer Kulturbesitz / Art Resource, NY

103. Golden Splendor

Try this palette if you want to go all out with gold (see a photo of the three on page 9). Not visible in print are the three different finishes of the gold beads—24kt metallic, alabaster, and matte—which create textural intrigue. **Delicas: DB-031, DB-621, DB-331a**

FINISHED LENGTH: LONGEST STRAND APPROXIMATELY 31"

Materials
• size .13 bead stringing wire (comes packaged in a standard length)
• 20 gms size 11o 25k gold-plated seed beads
• three 16" strands 4mm Czech metallic fire polished, pale gold
• four 16" strands 6mm Czech metallic fire polished, pale gold
• three 16" strands 8mm Czech metallic fire polished, pale gold
• four 16" strands 6 x 3mm Czech pressed square melon, topaz AB
• two 16" strands 7mm Czech pressed coin, topaz AB
• two 16" strands 10mm Czech pressed coin, topaz AB
• two 16" strands 14 x 4mm Czech pressed tubes, topaz AB
• one 16" strand 16 x 5mm Czech flat triangle daggers, topaz AB
• twelve crimp beads, vermeil or gold
• one 12-strand clasp
• two 12-strand spacer bars
• circular foam core armature (see diagram, next page)

Tools
• crimping tool
• wire cutters

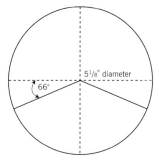

Circular armature
Permission is granted to photocopy this template. To use as an armature, enlarge 200%, glue to $1/4$" thick foam core, and cut out. Paste onto a $10 1/2$" x $10 1/2$" piece of foam core base. Lay strands around the disk.

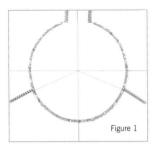

Figure 1

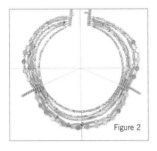

Figure 2

The first row, the one closest to the inside of the neck, will be the shortest strand. Including spacer bars, clasps, and crimp beads, this strand will be 15" or 16" long, depending on how wide you would like the necklace. Mine is 16" long and fits gently around an average sized neck. The spacer bars on this 16" strand are 4¾" from each end of the strand, and fall at a 66 degree angle from the center horizontal line. The circular armature used in figure 1 is 5⅛" wide. I've left 1" of space between the clasps.

String a sequence of the smallest beads on the first strand. I alternated the 4mm faceted rounds with the 6 x 3mm square melons while nestling a gold seed bead between each. For visual consistency and textural interest, use a gold seed bead between each bead on the entire piece. Finish all ends using crimp beads as described on page 170.

With the piece laying flat around the circular armature, string each consecutive strand slightly longer than the previous one. Keep tension consistent. I find it easiest to cut the beading wire about 4" longer than necessary and hold one end taut with tape or a bead stopper. I work one strand at a time, leaving both ends loose until I'm sure of the placement of each bead on the entire strand. Because every strand is different its impossible to get each of the three segments perfectly symmetrical, so aim for visual symmetry. You may have to place an extra seed bead here and there to occupy the space needed to make each strand the correct length (figure 2).

Figure 3

GENERAL GUIDELINES FOR THE STRINGING PATTERN:

- String a seed bead between every larger bead.
- After exiting each opening of the clasp string a crimp bead, a seed bead, one 4mm faceted round, and a seed bead (figure 3).
- Flank every opening of the spacer bars with a seed bead and one 4mm faceted round (figure 4).
- Use smallest beads on first four strands; medium-sized beads on next 4 strands; and largest beads on last four strands.
- Alternate dagger beads and 8mm faceted rounds (seed beads between each!) on the last strand.
- When stringing dagger beads be mindful of which side of the bead faces out. You may want to alternate the iridescent finished side with the non-finished side.

Try this as a five-strand necklace in other colors.

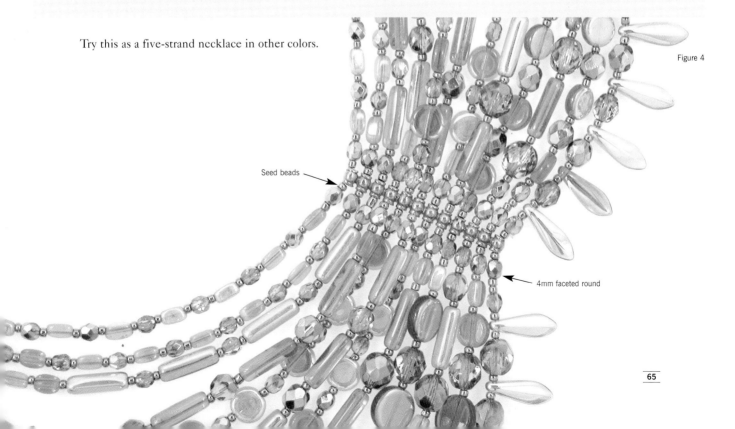

Figure 4

Seed beads

4mm faceted round

Minoan Embroidered Pendant

Designed and created by Heidi Kummli

How-to photographs by Heidi Kummli

ADVANCED

Use metal stampings of your own making, as Heidi has done, or select gemstone cabochons to create a focal point for a bead embroidered pendant.

104. Minoan Palette

At the north entrance to the Palace of Knossos, the colossal columns frame a richly saturated palette of brick red, intense sky blue, black, and sage green accented by bright goldenrod yellow. An extraordinarily sophisticated and daring color scheme. **Delicas: DB-773, DB-905, DB-310, DB-374, DB-651**

The bull mural of the Palace of Knossos provides color inspiration for Heidi Kummli's rich, earthy color scheme. A ring of goldenrod yellow, the brightest color, reinforces the focus, drawing the eye right to the center.

Materials
- three to five cabochons, metal stampings, or discs of your choice
- matching seed beads of your choice (Delicas, 11o and 14o sizes)
- matching colored Ultrasuede
- size B Nymo thread
- size 12 sharp needle
- poster board
- E6000 glue
- Tacky Glue
- bead loom
- braided leather cord
- end caps and clasp

Tool
- scissors

Using your largest stone, disc, or metal stamping as a focal point, arrange the other stones and stampings around it in a way that appeals to you (figure 1). Symmetrical designs are easiest to work with.

Cut a piece of Ultrasuede at least 1" larger than the perimeter of your cabochon/stone arrangement.

Choose no more than three colors of seed beads for a project this size to avoid creating a chaotic and busy appearance.

Using E6000, glue the largest stone to the Ultrasuede. Allow the glue to set up for a least 30 minutes.

You will be using the backstitch to attach seed beads to the Ultrasuede. Thread a knot on one end of one yard of Nymo thread; thread a needle on the other end. Push the needle up through the back of the suede, exiting on the top right next to the focal stone. Add six seed beads, lay them next to the stone so they lay snug but not bunched up. Push your needle back down through the suede right next to the last bead you threaded. Bring needle back up between the third and fourth bead. Sew

Figure 1

through the last three beads. Repeat until you have circled the whole stone with a row of beads. If necessary, adjust the number of beads at the end by adding or subtracting one or two. Thread back through the whole row to tighten the beads against the stone.

Push your needle up a bead's width away from the first row and create a second row exactly as you did the first. Alternate colors to make a pattern, as shown in the photo (left). When you get to the end of the row sew back through all the beads like you did on the first row. Don't pull too tight this time or the beads will bunch up too close to the first row (figure 2). Repeat for the third row.

Figure 2

Using the E6000, glue another stone in place. Add as many rows of beads as necessary to surround the remaining stones or add additional rows as shown.

Once you have finished surrounding the stones and filling in spaces with seed beads trim off the excess Ultrasuede with scissors (figure 3). Be careful not to cut any existing threads. Leave 1/8" of Ultrasuede to sew your beaded edging upon.

Making a Bail

Using Delica beads on a seed bead loom, weave a 12-bead x 22-bead strip (see pages 178–179). If you prefer, construct a bail using an off-loom weaving stitch.

Figure 3

Figure 4

Fold a piece of masking tape around the warp threads on each side next to the beadwork to make flaps (figure 4). Fold the woven strip in half, lining each end row together, and glue the two flaps together using Tacky Glue.

To create a stiff backing, lay your finished piece on a piece of poster board and trace around it. Cut the poster board 1/8" smaller than your finished piece.

Center the folded bail at the top back of the Ultra-suede and glue it in place using Tacky Glue (figure 5).

Apply Tacky Glue to the poster board backing, and glue it to the back of the Ultrasuede, sandwiching the bail in between (figure 6). Lay the whole piece onto another piece of Ultrasuede and trace around it. Cut this piece of suede a little larger than your finished piece.

Glue this to the back of your finished piece. You now have a three layer sandwich, with poster board backing in the middle. Press the top of your finished piece onto the suede making sure the beads are all lying flat. Let glue dry 15 minutes and trim off the excess suede.

Figure 5

Figure 6

Finishing the Edges

A seed beaded edging keeps the finished pieces of the sandwich sewn together and provides a professional finish to the edges.

Tie a knot at the end of one yard of Nymo thread and thread a needle on the other end. Push the needle up in between the two layers of suede to hide the knot. Exit on the top of the piece next to the bail.

Add four beads (figure 7). Push the needle up from the back to the front, about 1/8" from where your needle last exited, threading it through the last bead you added. Repeat this along the entire edge. When you reach the other side of the bail, edge right over it pushing the needle through the masking tape and backing. This reinforces the bail.

If necessary, adjust the remaining number of beads to make the edging even. Sew back through the first bead and push the needle through to the back. Knot the thread three times next to the suede backing. Push the needle up through the suede and cut the thread. Clean up with a damp cotton swab.

Hang your embroidered pendant from neck wire, neck ring, cable, or cord of your choice.

Figure 7

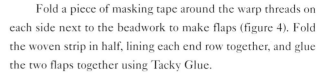

CULTURES OF OUR WORLD

Traditional Huichol beadwork, with its bright, saturated colors, speaks the bold rhythms and colors of Latin America.

Strong, bright, multi-colored fabrics work beautifully with dense black.

Typical Huichol beaded mask made by Huichol people of Mexico.

LATIN AMERICA

Each Latin country has its bounty of spectacular colors and combinations. From Mexico all the way down to the southernmost tip of South America, the colors vibrate and sing. People paint their homes bright orange and pink. They stripe their blankets with Crayola-like colors, and there's little backing off—most hues are at full strength! Softened cameo tones can be found, yet even the calmer tones are combined into bold high contrast schemes. It's a world alive with sizzling, festive colors.

Window in La Boca, Buenos Aires

105. La Boca

As you grow bolder with your choices you become a color sophisticate. These Latin palettes are the ones to cut your teeth on. A window in La Boca, Buenos Aires (left) gives us this playful palette. Pull out all the stops with this one and have fun. Add more shades of pink and lemony greens and let go. **Delicas: DB-215, DB-914, DB-274**

CULTURES OF OUR WORLD

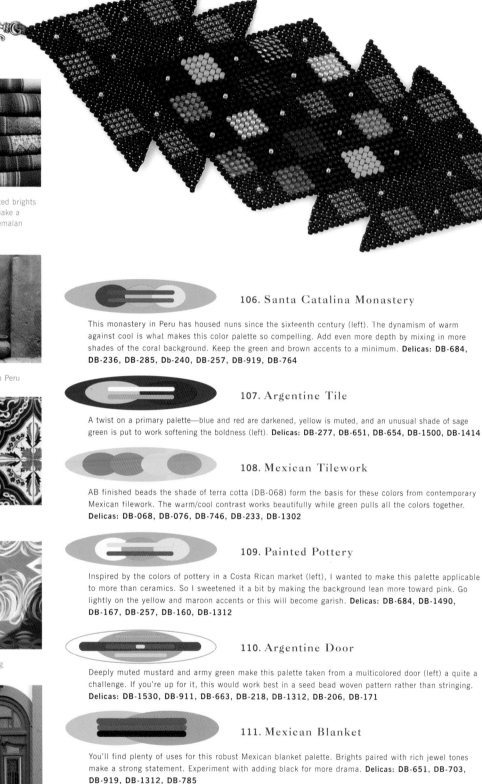

Margie Deeb weaves saturated brights against a field of black to make a bracelet inspired by a Guatemalan blanket. Brickstitch

Santa Catalina Monastery in Peru

Argentine tile

Costa Rican pottery painting

A colorfully-painted Argentinean door

106. Santa Catalina Monastery

This monastery in Peru has housed nuns since the sixteenth century (left). The dynamism of warm against cool is what makes this color palette so compelling. Add even more depth by mixing in more shades of the coral background. Keep the green and brown accents to a minimum. **Delicas: DB-684, DB-236, DB-285, Db-240, DB-257, DB-919, DB-764**

107. Argentine Tile

A twist on a primary palette—blue and red are darkened, yellow is muted, and an unusual shade of sage green is put to work softening the boldness (left). **Delicas: DB-277, DB-651, DB-654, DB-1500, DB-1414**

108. Mexican Tilework

AB finished beads the shade of terra cotta (DB-068) form the basis for these colors from contemporary Mexican tilework. The warm/cool contrast works beautifully while green pulls all the colors together. **Delicas: DB-068, DB-076, DB-746, DB-233, DB-1302**

109. Painted Pottery

Inspired by the colors of pottery in a Costa Rican market (left), I wanted to make this palette applicable to more than ceramics. So I sweetened it a bit by making the background lean more toward pink. Go lightly on the yellow and maroon accents or this will become garish. **Delicas: DB-684, DB-1490, DB-167, DB-257, DB-160, DB-1312**

110. Argentine Door

Deeply muted mustard and army green make this palette taken from a multicolored door (left) a quite a challenge. If you're up for it, this would work best in a seed bead woven pattern rather than stringing. **Delicas: DB-1530, DB-911, DB-663, DB-218, DB-1312, DB-206, DB-171**

111. Mexican Blanket

You'll find plenty of uses for this robust Mexican blanket palette. Brights paired with rich jewel tones make a strong statement. Experiment with adding black for more drama. **Delicas: DB-651, DB-703, DB-919, DB-1312, DB-785**

112. Happy Harmony

Cheerful colors with similar value are often easy to work with. This chipper array, inspired by a stack of brightly painted apartments in Argentina, delivers plenty of color but little value contrast. Use all colors in unrestrained portions. **Delicas: DB-057, DB-233, DB-237, DB-077, DB-1302**

Heidi Kummli works the colors of this quaint Brazilian cafe in Paraná into her bead embroidered *Cranes*. Turquoise, and glass, hand-painted abalone from Russia, fossil clamshell hash by Gary Wilson, polymer clay cranes by Janis Holler of Loco Lobo designs. Photograph by Heidi Kummli

INDIA, NEPAL & TIBET

In parts of India, single colors, punctuated by architectural accents, unify entire cities. Jaisalmer, built of yellow sandstone, is the "golden city." Most buildings in Jodhpur, the "blue city," are painted blue. And Jaipur, the "pink city," uses ochre pink plasters to color its walls.

India is a world of color with fabrics sporting daring blends of reds, pinks, saffrons, yellows, blues, and greens. Men wear brightly colored turbans, and women's saris are spectral extravaganzas.

Tibetan culture and religion offer splendid colors, many wrought in intricately detailed patterns, like the fabrics draping the inside walls of monasteries. Traditional Tibetan dress relies heavily on forest green, maroon, and black, accented with cobalt blue and fuchsia.

Heavily influenced by the cultures of Tibet and India, Nepal is a land of elaborately colorful festivals, which bind together diverse Hindu and Buddhist backgrounds.

Coral, turquoise, and cowry shell is typical of jewelry in Nepal and Tibet.

Powdered pigments on sale in an Indian marketplace (above right) inspired the brilliant palette for *Twined Neon*, a loomed necklace designed by Margie Deeb. Loomwork by Frieda Bates

Jeweltones of Indian saris

113. India Pink

Vivid pink creates a striking backdrop for sumptuous jewel tones like those of the sari worn by local women (left). Add 24kt gold accents and you'll have an elegant, head-turning color scheme that's versatile and easy to work with. **Delicas: DB-247, DB-610, DB-281, DB-909, DB-031**

The mosque interior of the Taj Mahal inspired SaraBeth Cullinan to create *Beledi*, a necklace using shades of pink and detailed, intricate filigree. The green of the distant trees finds its way into the necklace as small pearl accents.
Glass and vermeil

Kal Bhairab statue in Durbar Square, Kathmandu, Nepal

An Indian batik

114. Kal Bhairab

Bright, straight-from-the- tube colors adorn the statue of Kal Bhairab, the Nepalese God of Destruction, at his temple in Kathmandu (left). Removed from the ferocious figure, this palette becomes festive, and its bold colors call for clean lines and simple details. **Delicas: DB-721, DB-010, DB-656, DB-730, DB-651, DB-200, DB-245**

115. Rajasthani Peacock

This elegant and feminine palette is taken from a blue and coral colored wall decoration featuring a peacock, a symbol of Rajasthan. Silver-lined matte finishes dominate, and a matte gold enhances the overall smooth surface finish of the whole palette. **Delicas: DB-696, DB-167, DB-684, DB-687, DB-331**

116. Warm and Bright

In India, palettes based on neutrals often include reds or maroons. Even though they are built on less saturated colors, they maintain the bold sophistication typical of Indian color schemes. This harmonious combination comes from batik fabric with elephant designs (left). **Delicas: DB-762, DB-764, DB-272, DB-274, DB-378**

Tibetan mandala

117. Tibetan Mandala

For Tibetan Buddhists, a mandala (above) is an imaginary palace that is contemplated during meditation. Colors represent the four elements and directions. Try weaving your own mandala of seed beads using this rainbow-like spectrum. **Delicas: DB-691, DB-167, DB-161, DB-160, DB-295, DB-010, DB-201**

118. Jodhpur Blues

A portion of Jodhpur paints many of its structures blue (below). Inspired by the landscape I've chosen three shades of similar blues as a background, and introduced warmth and vitality with salmon and pine green accents. This can also be achieved with blue lace agate or chalcedony, rhodonite, and jade. **Delicas: DB-361, DB-881, DB-1537, DB-207, DB-690**

119. Sri Meenakshi Temple

Covered with stucco figures of deities and mythical animals painted in vivid colors, the Meenakshi Sundareswarar Temple (below) is one of the most famous Hindu temples. This palette of five colors and white derives from a section of one of the towers. The beads are mostly pearl finishes. In gemstones, an array of chalcedonies and agates will achieve a similar luminous effect. **Delicas: DB-057, DB-236, DB-232, DB-237, DB-902**

120. The Robes

Bathed in warmth, this rich palette of saffron, red, and maroon comprises the colors of the Tibetan monks' robes. Amber, carnelian, and garnet can create vigorous drama; try using them with a trio of seed beads. **Delicas: DB-651, DB-654, DB-296**

City of Jodhpur

Sri Meenakshi Temple

Tibetans value turquoise second only to gold. Jean Campbell draws on the coral/turquoise/silver tradition of Himalayan craftsmen.
Flat and tubular peyote stitch, stringing, wirework

©iStockphoto.com / Peeter Viisimaa

AFRICA

Earth colors—those of sand, soil, and rock—are the heartbeat of Africa's cultural palettes. Alongside ochres, siennas, and umbers, bright colors pulse in rhythm. Red, as vital as blood, courses through many of these muscular color schemes, making them as forceful as they are substantial. Warmth, reflecting the heat of the continent, pervades all color schemes, from kente cloth, beaded collars, woodcarvings, and bright geometric exterior murals in the south, to the ornate tile work and architecture in the north. The colors of Africa are primitive, sophisticated, raw, vibrant, elegant, and passionate.

Madrona-Tree Protection Goddess wears the strength of an African palette: primal red adorned with neutral tones. Robin Atkins embellished this fabric doll sculpture with bead embroidery featuring glass, pearls, and bone beads.
Photograph by Robin Atkins

121. Kente

Kente, a hand-woven ceremonial cloth (above), provides a visual representation of history, philosophy, ethics, oral literature, moral values, and code of conduct. Our contemporary palette features many colors, rather than the limited palettes of the older, traditional cloths.
Delicas: DB-378, DB-310, DB-651, DB-707, DB-730, DB-169, DB-655, DB-200

122. Embroidered Bag

Maroon, soft blue, and gentle yellow form a moderate version of the primary red-blue-yellow triad from an embroidered African bag (left). Accentuate the triad with small, precise dots of black and white. **Delicas:** DB-924, DB-240, DB-233, DB-310

Image licensed from PicturesNow.com

Embroidered African bag

CULTURES OF OUR WORLD

In *Regency*, Marcia DeCoster weaves rhythmic patterns in bold colors inspired by Kente cloth and drums. Black becomes the unifying beat as beaded beads meet textured yarn and lampworked glass.
Lampwork by Janice Peacock and Julie West of Leopard Heart Glass

Photo by Steven Ford, www.Fordesign.net

Young Masai woman

©iStockphoto.com / Chris Schmidt

Tunisian pottery

Photo by Ken Alexander

Women in Marrakech

123. Masai Beadwork

The Masai (left) use red as the dominant tone in most of their beadwork. Along with other bright colors, it stands out dramatically against neutral and dark backgrounds. This palette uses warm red leaning toward orange as a foundation for fully saturated, matte opaque finished colors.
Delicas: DB-757, DB-748, DB-200, DB-310, DB-754, DB-751

124. Fountain of Light

I've heightened the colors of a fountain covered by an Arabic mosaic by using AB finished beads and substituting gold for amber. Sparkle abounds in this cool, light pale palette. **Delicas: DB-052, DB-063, DB-076, DB-904, DB-031**

125. Tunisian Pottery

In a tradition hundreds of years old, Tunisian pottery (left) is turned by men and decorated by women. Using a wash of transparent bright colors on a mellowed earthen background, they embellish the surface with Islamic inspired geometric forms, arabesque foliate shapes, and intricate Spanish-Moorish details. **Delicas: DB-205, DB-076, DB-105, DB-917, DB-301**

126. Stroll Through Marrakech

The colors in the photo of the two women in Marrakech (bottom left) form an irresistible palette of warm, earth tones studded with brilliant accents. The proportion of brick orange to the other colors makes a dramatic presentation. Use this in a design that is as striking as the image. **Delicas: DB-1302, DB-762, DB-748, DB-169**

127. Berber Jewelry

Berber women from the Draa Valley in southern Morocco adorn themselves in a flamboyant array of silver, agate, branch coral, and amazonite. This bold palette simulates the look of some of the marvelous bracelets, necklaces, and hair ornaments they wear. **Delicas: DB-651, DB-653, DB-654, DB-166, DB-010**

128. The Sudan

A warm palette from across the plains or desert, and found on African wood carvings all over the continent. Topaz lifts the scheme with its light, and orange injects vitality. Matte finishes provide a chalky, dry, earthen texture. **Delicas: DB-312, DB-742, DB-795, DB-764, DB-310**

Pattern and texture abound in
African-inspired palettes. Women
of the Kikuyu tribe use earth
from the foothills of Mount Kenya
to form beautiful ceramic beads.
(Beads distributed by Some
Enchanted Beading.)
Necklace by Margie Deeb

African ceremonial mask

Yemen minaret

THE MIDDLE EAST

Madagascar jasper cabs cut by
Gary Wilson provide the focal point
for this muted mineral toned palette
by Mary Hicklin.
Peruvian blue opal, apatite, rutilated
quartz, pearls, sterling bezels, beads,
and findings; removable pendant

Selective palettes in subdued colors cover much of the Middle East. A variety of mineral tones dominate the various cultures, with earthy ochres playing the major role. Sun and sand influence architectural palettes; desert cities are often monochromatic, their walls fashioned out of the earth on which they rest. Among countless rows of baked brick structures, brightly painted doors offer the only color. Yemeni architecture trims its earth tones in decorative patterns of white lime.

The most forceful colors of The Middle East (other than the red of checkered head scarves worn by Saudi men) are the deepened reds of carpets, and the blacks, whites, and indigo blues sanctioned for decorous dress.

The tile colors in monuments are an exception to sober palettes. In these geometric patterns we find cobalt blues, aquas, bright yellows, maroons, and greens, unified by white. When mosaics cover the domed mosques, they shimmer like jewels in the sky.

Because so many colors mellow into shades and earth tones prevail, there is an overall consonance and harmony to the subdued palettes of the Middle East.

Rainbow Calcite Cilica Set
Cinnabar red unifies a bright earth-based palette like that of these Turkish scarves. Bead embroidered necklace and earring set by Elizabeth Ann Scarborough. Rainbow calcite, glass beads

©iStockphoto.com/Erik de Graaf

Islamic mosaic

129. Mosaic of Color

An Islamic mosaic (left) brings together a wide range of hues softened in tone. Matte finishes dominate our bead palette, with the exceptions of the main blue-green (DB-217) and goldenrod (DB-651), which are opaque with reflective surfaces. **Delicas: DB-217, DB-361, DB-762, DB-779, DB-651, DB-776**

130. Woven is Me

Companionable colors from an elaborately detailed woven rug are as balanced as they are beautiful. The quiet palette has an inherent sense of harmony united through tonally well matched hues. **Delicas: DB-852, DB-376, DB-371, DB-388, DB-1302, DB-311, DB-361**

131. Tranquil Blue

Blues set the tone of this soothing palette borrowed from a prayer carpet in an Istanbul mosque. Accents of a very yellowed avocado green bring it to life. Create this harmony in gemstones using sodalite, blue chalcedony, and serpentine. **Delicas: DB-726, DB-361, DB-240, DB-388, DB-371**

Instanbul tile work

132. Cool Blue Tile

Tilework in Istanbul (left) presents a refreshing combination of cool blues on a pearl white field accented with a flourish of red. The original tiles feature an ornate rhythmical floral pattern that lets much of the white show through, giving a feeling of light and space. **Delicas: DB-201, DB-730, DB-1497, DB-861, DB-707, DB-727**

The power in Kim price's multi-strand comes from carnelian the color of Turkish carpets.
Quartz, pearls, glass charlottes, and silver

Brick and whitewash of Yemen

Oman residence

133. Brick and Whitewash

Yemen is famous for its elegant mud-brick houses (left) pierced by arched windows and decorated with geometric designs in whitewash or pale stone. Notice the pure green of the window's geometric ornamentation. **Delicas: DB-773, DB-1302, DB-312, DB-201, DB-776**

134. Cool in the Desert

Though it's not the dominant color, this house in Oman (bottom left) uses blue as a focal point. On a background of cream, all three colors stand out, articulating and defining the design. The tension between warm and cool in this palette is exquisite. **Delicas: DB-352, DB-726, DB-1480, DB-764**

135. Turkish Carpet

Known for their luxurious deep red-oranges, Turkish carpets employ a panoply of elegant muted tones. Like most of their palettes, this one reaches an ideal balance of temperature, hue, and value. One of the secrets to achieving such balance is found in accenting with the lightest light and darkest dark, while allowing mid-tones to dominate. **Delicas: DB-773, DB-781, DB-361, DB-353, DB-311**

136. Mauve Magic

This contemplative palette, inspired by a scarf in a Jerusalem market, begins with gorgeous muted lavender and mauve-pink tones. Dove-gray softens them even more. A slice of gunmetal gray (DB-001), the strongest tone in the group, prevents monotony. The semi-matte silver lined finishes mimic satin and heighten the elegance. **Delicas: DB-629, DB-1413, DB-1456, DB-001**

In *Yang Collar*, Joan Babcock uses restrained tones and a miniscule amount of red to accentuate the focal pendant. Cavandoli knotting, brass, silver, and glass beads

Image licensed from PicturesNow.com

THE FAR EAST

All kinds of palettes find a home in the Far East. Aiming for harmony with the environment, sober grays and wood tones inhabit traditional Japanese architecture, and festive brilliant colors dance on Chinese lanterns and dragons. Primary colors and gold encrust shrines in Bangkok, while Mandalay's temples gleam white against verdant foliage. Earthen muted schemes embellish Thai and Cambodian silks.

Red plays a sovereign role in most eastern cultures, and is found in architecture, fabrics and interiors, as well as dance, and theater costumes and sets.

©iStockphoto.com / Christine Gonsalves

Margie Deeb creates a classic Chinese color scheme, like the one from a temple (left). Chinese porcelain and glass

Japanese silk painting

Thai Demon of the Grand Palace

137. Japanese Silk Painting

The colors of traditional silks and woodcut prints are often formed on neutral backgrounds Rather than copy the colors from a typical Japanese silk painting (above left), I've distilled the essence of the palette: neutrals, black, and whispers of pink and blue. **Delicas: DB-1520, DB-205, DB-310, DB-749, DB-902, DB-218**

138. Thai Demons

Gold abounds in the Grand Palace complex in Bangkok, the seat of power and spiritual heart of Thailand. Brightly colored mosaics cover buildings and statues, like this demon (above right). The palette includes silver (DB-032), which is actually a white gold. Treat the brightest colors and silver as accents. Surround everything in gold. **Delicas: DB-031, DB-729, DB-705, DB-707, DB-704, DB-032**

139. Balinese Dancers

Known for their luxurious deep red-oranges, Turkish carpets employ a panoply of elegant muted tones. Like most of their palettes, this one reaches an ideal balance of temperature, hue, and value. One of the secrets to achieving such balance is found in accenting with the lightest light and darkest dark, while allowing mid-tones to dominate. **Delicas: DB-283, DB-031, DB-331, DB-001, DB-919**

140. Canary and Peony

Elegant and feminine, low-intensity tones dictate this palette inspired by a Japanese woodcut from the 1800s. The cool blues and greens provide soft contrast to sparks of orange, which boost the vitality. Because the background blue is matte, the other surface finishes sparkle all the more. **Delicas: DB-798, DB-919, DB-1484, DB-913, DB-106, DB-1479**

The contemporary, refined palette of *Santa F'Asian*, by Joan Babcock, exhibits the colors of a structure in a Japanese garden.

Saffron yellow and a range of reds reflect the palette of many Far East temples like this one in Thailand.
Glass bead necklace by Carol Cypher

CULTURES OF OUR WORLD

Laotian temple doors

Boat in floating Thai market

141. Temple Doors

The doors to this Laotian temple (left) use a simple yet stunning palette: crimson and gold. In beads, we give it a twist by using both a highly reflective 24kt gold and a matte finished gold. Varying surface finish of the same color adds dimension and texture to finished work. **Delicas: DB-1312, DB-031, DB-331**

142. Boat Market

The bright colors in the photo of a woman selling fruit from her boat at a floating market in Thailand (left) inspired this fresh, vibrant scheme. Three AB finishes provide an extra flourish of color. **Delicas: DB-281, DB-160, DB-174, DB-161, DB-1491**

143. Cambodian Dancers

How odd to combine a cool teal green with hot citrus colors of orange and lime, but it works! Look at the Delicas suggested and you'll see how the shimmering surfaces enhance the compelling harmony of these colors worn by traditional male dancers in the Cambodian Cultural Village in the Siem Reap district. **Delicas: DB-151, DB-043, DB-910, DB-238**

144. Japanese Silk

Vivid and low-intensity tones comprise the gorgeous analogous palette taken from a maple leaf design woven into Japanese silk. The force of red is softened by the grays and the dark, neutralized orange (DB-773). In gemstones, use carnelians, amber, and hematite. **Delicas: DB-683, DB-703, DB-773, DB-761, DB-233**

Multi-strand Seed Bead Bracelet

Designed and created by Margie Deeb

E A S Y

> A lavish and elegant 27-strand cuff bracelet in sophisticated colors is easier to make than you might think. Making each strand the exact length is the biggest challenge; distributing the accent colors is the most fun!

145. Thai Murals

These soft muted colors harmonize beautifully together. Use whichever one you want as a dominant. In the bracelet project, brown serves as a wonderfully neutral dominant color upon which the others thrive. **Delicas: DB-376, DB-374, DB-327, DB-208, DB-322, DB-764, DB-031**

FINISHED LENGTH: TWENTY-SEVEN 7" TO 8" STRANDS, DEPENDING ON FINDING AND CLOSUR

Materials
- forty-four size 8o seed beads, matte metallic bronze
- 1 gm size 11o seed beads, gold
- 2 gms size 11o seed beads, light peach
- 2 gms size 11o seed beads, dusty rose
- 3 gms size 11o seed beads, matte metallic bronze
- 3 gms size 11o seed beads, olive green
- 8 gms size 11o seed beads, pale blue
- 4 gms size 11o seed beads, sage green
- accent beads: twenty 4mm faceted rounds, gold luster finished rust
- accent beads: thirty 3mm saucer or round beads, gold
- gold or vermeil 3-strand finding with clasp (hook, toggle, or magnetic)
- size 11 or 12 beading needle
- size D Nymo thread, ash

Margie Deeb's multi-strand bracelet uses accents of gold and terra cotta to punctuate an array of gently muted tones from the Thai wall painting in the Temple of the Reclining Buddah.

Photo by Allison O'Neill

The black in the inspiration piece was omitted from the bead color palette. In the painting, black visually separates areas of color, making the scenes easier to "read." For the bracelet, however, it's not necessary, nor would it be appealing.

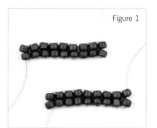

Figure 1

Thread needle with 36" of Nymo. Using the size 8o seed beads, make two, 2-drop, brick stitch "ladders" 9 stacks wide, one for the foundation of each end of the bracelet (see page 176). Enforce them by looping the thread through each end a couple of times. Don't clip the tails, leave them long, for you will use them later (figure 1.)

You will add four rows of decreasing brick stitch to each of these ladders after the bracelet strands are finished. They will then be 1⁹/₁₆" high. Place the two foundation ladders 4³/₄" apart.

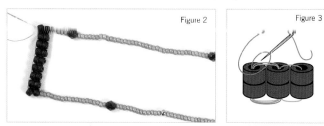

Figure 2

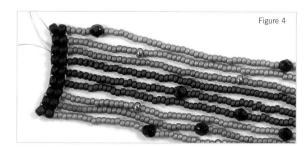

Figure 3

String two blue strands, one from each end ladder to end, connecting one ladder to the other. Be sure these two strands are exactly the same length. The two ladders should be parallel to each other (figure 2). String random accents of the gold 3mm and rust 4mm beads. Knot the working thread onto the top of the ladder by passing the needle under the connecting thread between two ladder beads, then through the loop that is created before you pull it all the way through (figure 3). You are now ready to string all 27 strands.

Stringing Tips

- Make each strand the same length, keeping the foundation ladders parallel. This is tricky, and some strands will inevitably end up being a bit longer than others. However, once the bracelet is wrapped around a wrist (figure 7), the varying lengths will not be visible.

- Place one to four accent beads per strand, making sure they do not align with other accents beads.

- Knot the thread (figure 3) as often as possible. You'll eventually conceal the knots and the thread along the top of the ladder by adding more rows of 8o bronze beads to the ladder.

Figure 4

- String one strand per foundation stack until you have nine strands (figure 4). Then work your way back to the beginning, stringing a second strand in each foundation stack. Then string a third strand coming from each foundation stack. Follow the color chart in figure 5, placing one gold strand in the center, exiting foundation stack #5.

Using basic brick stitch, add four more rows to each foundation ladder.

Attach the 3-strand finding as shown in figure 6, passing and wrapping the thread through the holes as many times as possible, and alternating the bead from which it exits.

Run thread through the foundation to tie off, and clip tail. Use a brown permanent marker (Sharpies work well) to stain unsightly threads that shown in the foundation sections.

Figure 5

| 1 | 2 | 3 | 4 | 5 | 6 | 7 | 8 | 9 |

Figure 6

Figure 7

Festival of Fringe Necklace

Designed and created by Margie Deeb

INTERMEDIATE

> Nineteen brightly colored strands hang from a woven ring of size 8o beads. The uniform, symmetrical arrangement of quick color and value changes unifies what could have been an unpleasantly chaotic piece.

146. Guatemalan Festival

Don't be daunted by this wide-ranging palette. If you keep red as the obvious dominant color, and stick to the proportions shown, you can't go wrong. They're all brights, and with black as an accent, whatever you make will be exciting. **Delicas: DB-745, DB-247, DB-160, DB-174, DB-705, DB-076, DB-165, DB-310**

The inspiration for my bead palette was this traditional Guatemalan cloth from the Mam Indians. I added orange because I like the light and the zesty flavor it added. The wide range of colors and contrast make this piece lively and engaging.

FINISHED LENGTH: 14³/4" CHOKER, 5³/4" CENTER FRINGE STRAND

Materials

- size 8o transparent seed beads (substitute opaque if necessary), 5-10gms each of the following colors: red, orange, yellow, cobalt blue, aqua blue, lime green, emerald green, magenta
- size 8o black matte opaque beads, 5gms
- assorted fringe beads, at least 20 of each
- 2 size 6o red seed beads
- Nymo size D thread, ash color
- clasp

Foundation Choker

Create the choker in the tubular herringbone stitch begun on a bead ladder. Using Nymo thread and red 8o seed beads, begin by making a ladder four beads wide (figure 1). Leave a 9" tail that you will use to connect to the clasp. Connect the ends to create a box by weaving down through bead #1, up through bead #4, and back down through bead #1, and up through bead #2 (figure 2).

Add two beads (#5 and #6) and go down through either bead #3 (if you like to work right to left), or bead #1 (if you prefer to work left to right). In the illustrations, we are working left to right, so the needle will pass down through bead #1 (figure 3).

Pass needle up through bead #4. Add two beads (#7 and #8) and go down through bead #3. Go up through bead #2 and #5; add two beads (#9 and #10) and go down through bead #6 only (the top of the neighboring stack), exiting between beads #6 and #1 (figure 4).

| Figure 1 | Figure 2 | Figure 3 | Figure 4 |

Pass needle up through bead #7. Add two beads (#11 and #12) and pass down through bead #8 only, the bead at the top of the neighboring stack. From now on you will work your way around the box, adding two beads and passing down through only the top bead of each neighboring stack. Continue, following the color pattern shown in figure 5, until you've made a choker your desired length minus the length of the clasp (mine is $13^1/2$" long).

Fringe

Begin creating the fringe in the center of the choker, in this case, aligned with the yellow row.

Tie on a new thread that is as long as you can comfortably use, and work your way to the center of the choker, exiting to either the right or the left of the center bead. Add a variety of different shaped and sized beads separated by the 8o beads used on the choker, creating a strand 5" to 6" long. Add a stop bead at the bottom, then sew back up through the whole strand. Pass through two choker beads and exit (figure 6.) Create another strand that is slightly shorter than the center strand. Create an identical strand on the opposite side (figure 7). Continue back and forth this way, adding a few strands on each side, then the other, checking for visual balance and symmetry of the strands. I strung the largest of all fringe beads at the bottom of each strand, adding weight and panache to the composition. When working your thread back and forth between strands, slide it through other choker rows if you need to. But be sure that each strand of fringe hangs from the same row of the choker.

Make nine strands on either side of the center strand to create a total of nineteen strands.

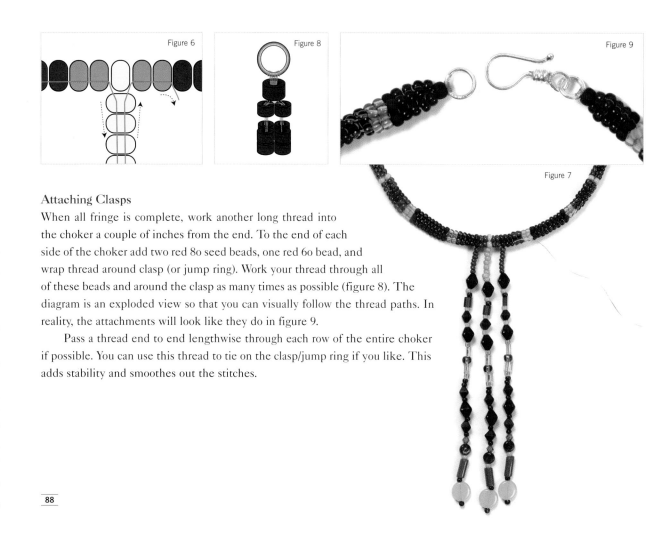

Figure 5

Figure 6

Figure 8

Figure 9

Figure 7

Attaching Clasps

When all fringe is complete, work another long thread into the choker a couple of inches from the end. To the end of each side of the choker add two red 8o seed beads, one red 6o bead, and wrap thread around clasp (or jump ring). Work your thread through all of these beads and around the clasp as many times as possible (figure 8). The diagram is an exploded view so that you can visually follow the thread paths. In reality, the attachments will look like they do in figure 9.

Pass a thread end to end lengthwise through each row of the entire choker if possible. You can use this thread to tie on the clasp/jump ring if you like. This adds stability and smoothes out the stitches.

Collar of Glass & Light

Designed and created by Margie Deeb

Strands of dagger beads arranged to look like leaves encircle a gold tubular herringbone foundation, creating a wreath of sparkling color. The supple, soft texture of this necklace feels more like fabric than glass.

The Dome of the Rock, which was built over 1,300 years ago, dominates the skyline of Jerusalem. The sparkling blues, greens, and gold of its tile and glass inspired this beaded collar.

©iStockphoto.com / Terry J Alcorn

FINISHED LENGTH: 13" TO 15", DEPENDING ON FINDING AND CLOSURE

Materials
- 10 gms size 11o seed beads, 24k gold plated
- sixty-five 16mm x 5mm dagger beads, transparent cobalt
- sixty-five 16mm x 5mm dagger beads, vitrail
- sixty-five 16mm x 5mm dagger beads, seafoam/white
- sixty-five 16mm x 5mm dagger beads, turquoise
- forty-eight 16mm x 5mm dagger beads, light aqua
- seventeen 16mm x 5mm dagger beads, emerald green AB
- two size 6o or 8o seed beads, gold
- size 11 or 12 beading needle
- size B Nymo thread, ash
- gold or gold plated clasp and finding

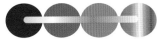

147. Dome of the Rock

An analogous range of cool liquid colors—blue, turquoise, and green—are juxtaposed against flashes of hard metallic highlights. The overall effect is sumptuous and compelling. **Delicas: DB-707, DB-113, DB-705, DB-032, DB-031**

Foundation Choker

Using Nymo B thread and size 11o gold-plated beads, create a choker in tubular herringbone stitch as shown on page 87–88 (figures 1, 2, 3, 4, and 5) your desired length minus the length of the clasp (mine is 13^1/$_2$").

Fringe

Tie on a new thread that is as long as you can comfortably use. Leave a tail you will either weave back in or use to attach the clasp with later.

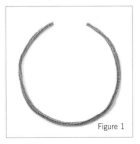

Figure 1

Figure 2

Light passes through the transparent beads and bounces off the AB and metallic finishes, creating a dazzling display of textural luminosity. String accents of the darker teal green on every 4th or 5th fringe strand, replacing the light aqua dagger bead.

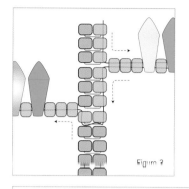

Figure 2

Exit between two beads that are four to five rows in from the end of the choker. Add three gold seed beads. Now alternate between adding a dagger bead of each color (except the emerald AB accent beads), and a gold seed bead (figure 2). String a gold seed bead for a stop bead and pass back through the fringe and down into the same column of the choker that you exited to make this strand of fringe. Pass through four gold beads and exit. Pass your needle underneath the thread within the choker that connects the two columns at that point, following the thread path in figure 3. (Looping around the connecting choker thread is an important step, as it makes the fringe less likely to pull groups of herringbone rows together between the strands.) You will follow this thread path between each of the sixty-five strands of fringe that you make. Your fringe will hang from one side of the box-shape of the choker with each strand alternating between the left and the right-hand column (figure 4). A space of three seed beads will be between each strand.

Replace the palest transparent dagger bead with an emerald AB dagger on every fourth or fifth strand.

Figure 5

Attaching Clasps

When all sixty-five fringe strands are complete, tie off your working thread. Work another long thread into the choker a couple of inches from the end, and exit through one column of gold seed beads. Add one gold 6o or 8o seed bead to the end of the choker and wrap thread around clasp (or jump ring). Work your way back through the large seed bead and down into one of the three rows of herringbone you did not just exit from. Repeat until you have made a connection from each herringbone row up through the large seed bead and around the clasp. Do this as many times as possible, until the larger seed bead is full of thread. Thread through all of these beads and around the clasp until you can't pass through the larger seed beads anymore (figure 5). The diagram is an exploded view so that you can visually follow the thread paths. In reality, the attachments will look like they do in figure 6. Finish the other end in the same manner.

Pass a thread end to end lengthwise through each column of the entire choker if possible, tying off thread within the choker. This adds stability and straightens out the herringbone stitches.

Notice the necklace has a top and a bottom (figure 7). The front and back layers of fringe hang from this top creating depth.

Figure 7

Figure 6

Blended Multi-strand Necklace

Designed and created by Robin Atkins

How-to photographs by Robin Atkins

ADVANCED

This multi-strand necklace drapes beautifully and makes a significant statement when worn. When two colors are blended from side to side, the results are dramatic. The beads chosen for this design not only echo the colors of a traditional Japanese kimono, but also the patterns of the fabric. This is a versatile technique to showcase many beautiful, one-of-a-kind beads leftover from other projects.

148. Japanese Kimono

The most striking proportions of this perennial favorite are black as the dominant, red the secondary, and gold for accent colors. Using darkened red and matte gold provide a more sophisticated look than would a bright red and a highly reflective gold. **Delicas: DB-310, DB-654, DB-331**

Courtesan The drama of red, black, and gold is attention-getting in any setting in any culture. Inspired by the kimono colors, pattern, and form, Robin Atkins uses the popular combination of red, black, and gold.

FINISHED LENGTH: NINE STRANDS, RANGING FROM 28" TO 34"

Materials

- ¹/₂ oz. size 11o seed beads, opaque red
- 1 oz. size 11o seed beads, black (optional 3-cut)
- ¹/₂ oz. size 11o seed beads, opaque orange
- ¹/₂ oz. size 10o or 11o seed beads, transparent red-orange with AB finish
- approximately 2 oz. mixed accent beads of various sizes, black, red, orange
- five to fifteen mixed accent beads with gold embossing, especially fan shape
- 30–40 gms miscellaneous accent beads, various materials that look Japanese or Oriental (quantity depends on size of beads)
- four to eight accent beads, gold vermeil
- ten to twelve spacers
- bronze or gold vermeil clasp
- four crow beads, two black and two red
- number 18 bonded nylon upholstery thread, red
- size 00 or A fine Nymo beading thread, any color
- size 11 beading needle
- 36" x 18" (folded to 36" x 9" high) large piece medium-weight cotton beading cloth, off-white
- yardstick or measuring tape
- masking tape
- white glue, toothpick applicator
- black permanent marking pen

Lay out your beading cloth and apply a 36" strip of masking tape along the top edge. Measure and mark the center point on the tape. On each side of the center point measure and mark 14 inches and 17 inches. Your shortest strand will reach from one inside mark to the other (28 inches). The longest strand will reach from one outside mark to the other (34 inches). The other seven strands will be in regular increments between the longest and shortest strands.

Select beads that match the color scheme and reflect the Oriental nature of the project (figure 1). Place all beads on the beading cloth.

Figure 1

To create a harness for the upholstery thread upon which you will be adding beads, cut a 5" length of Nymo thread and thread it through the needle. Tie the two ends together in an overhand knot, leaving a loop with two 1" tails.

Cut a three-yard length of upholstery thread. Thread one end through the Nymo harness and double it back on itself for a double beading thread about 1½ yards long. Tie an overhand knot at the end, leaving 9" tails.

Lay out accent beads for this first strand. I begin with the shortest strand and work my way to the longest. Place black accent beads on the right-hand side of the strand; red on the left-hand side. Using the center mark on the tape as a guide for the focal area of your necklace, select fancier, larger accent beads for the center focal area, and space these beads fairly close together. Toward the ends of the strand space smaller accent beads increasingly further apart. String these accent beads with seed beads of appropriate colors between them. Check the length. Remove the harness, and tie a loose overhand knot at the loop end of the beading thread.

For each consecutive strand lay out and position accent beads between the accent beads on the previous strand (figure 2). String them with the seed beads. Continue in this way, until you have completed nine strands.

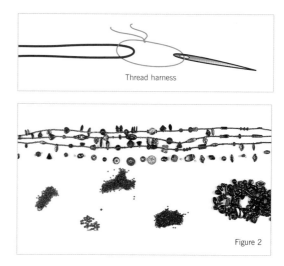

Thread harness

Figure 2

General guidelines for blending the black and red sides of the strands (figures 3, 4, and 5):

- Vary the placement of the color change from center to three inches either side of center.
- To gradually blend black to red, string one red, three black, one red, two black, one red, one black, two red, one black, three red, one black.
- Try the above formula using just seed beads.
- Try substituting an accent bead of the correct width for any grouping of same-color seed beads.
- Surprising, but true: you can randomly place a few red or red-orange accent beads on the black side and they will blend with the black. However, black accent beads on the red side stick out like a beader's sore thumb.
- Don't be overly concerned about the design of each individual strand. It's the overall look of all the strands together that is significant.

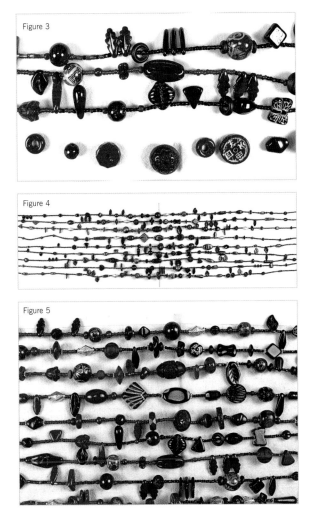

Figure 3

Figure 4

Figure 5

After all of the strands are complete, it's important to look at how they hang relative to each other. Gather the long loop ends on one side of the necklace, bundling them together just at the end of the beads. Tie a loose overhand knot right at the end of the strands. Check to be sure that none of the strands have slipped down exposing bare thread. Gather the cut tail ends at the other side of the necklace in the same way, and tie them together in an overhand knot. The strands of the necklace should now look exactly as they will once you have attached the clasp. Test the drape of the necklace by placing it around your neck or a form. Stand back and take a look.

Do any of the strands look bunched up or hang lopsided? Are there places where identical accent beads touch each other? In figure 6, the unadjusted version, there was a noticeable break between a group of shorter strands, which also looked "bunched up," and a group of longer strands. I could have left it that way, but don't you like the adjusted version (figure 7) better? The strands of this version hang at regularly spaced intervals, creating a neater appearance and showcasing the focal beads.

I write my adjustment notes on little strips of paper and tape them around the strands that need to be altered. Some strands need to be a tad longer, and I might write something like "add $1/2$" seed beads to red end." Other strands may need to be shortened by removing beads from one end or the other. When your notes are complete, untie the ending knots, and make adjustments. Before attaching the clasp, re-tie the ends, and take another look at how the strands hang. When you are satisfied it's time to finish your necklace.

Knotting is not a required step, however if you know how, knot each strand. I knot my strands about every three inches. You will need to tie a knot at each end of each strand, with at least nine inches of tails on both ends.

Gather all the threads on the red end and slip them through the harness. String two red crow beads and the hook part of the clasp. Insert the needle back into the second crow bead (figure 8), and pull all the threads through it. Remove the thread ends from the harness.

Adjust the assembly by pulling each thread until all of the strands are snug against the first crow bead. Check to be sure no seed beads have gotten into the hole of the first crow bead. Also check that there are no threads showing below the first crow bead (figure 9).

Create a loop by grasping the bundle of thread ends and bringing it under the two crow beads (figure 10). Lift the ends, placing them between the two crow beads, and insert them through the loop, forming an overhand knot (figure 11). Snug the knot, but don't tighten it completely. Make sure all strands are still snug against the first crow bead.

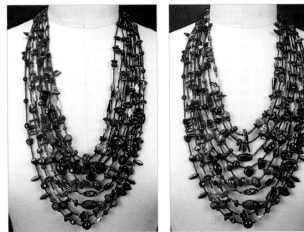

Figure 6

Figure 7

Tighten the knot by pulling gently on each thread individually. At this point, there should be no visible "blips" of thread showing in the knot. If there are, pull gently on each thread again. When the knot looks good, pull hard on each thread to make it as tight as possible (figure 12).

Use a toothpick to liberally apply the white glue, which dries transparent and slightly flexible, all over the knot (figure 13)

Insert all of the threads into the harness, insert the needle into the first crow bead (toward the strands), and pull all of the threads through (figure 14).

Remove the harness. Hold the threads away from the beaded strands and insert more glue, saturating all the threads in the first crow bead. Wipe excess glue from the crow bead with a damp tissue. Adjust the two crow beads so they are aligned (figure 15). Let the glue dry while you work with the other end of the strands.

Follow the same procedure for the "black end" of the necklace. Use a black permanent marker to color the last three inches of red thread on each of the strands before attaching jump ring part of the clasp. When the glue on both ends has completely dried, clip the threads right next to the crow bead. A curved finger nail scissors or a wire nipper works well for clipping them so close that they don't show (figure 16).

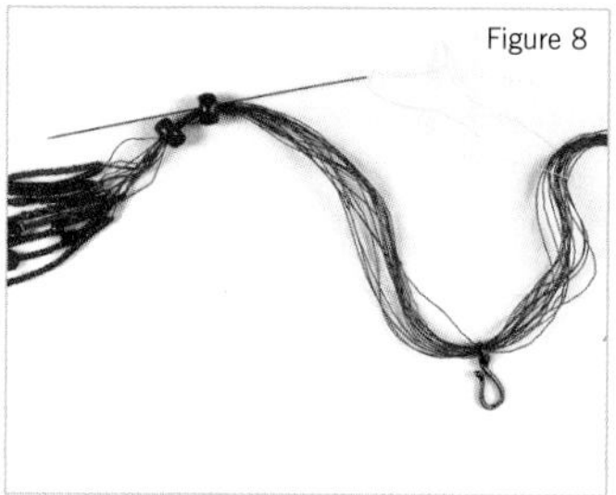

Figure 8

Figure 9

Figure 10

Figure 11

Figure 12

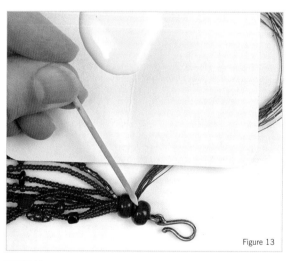

Figure 13

Feel free to vary these instructions according to your personal preferences. Nine is not a magic number. You can have as few as three or as many as 15 strands. The strands can be shorter or longer. They can all be the same length, which is nice if you want to twist the strands when you wear the necklace. Try increasing the space between the strands by increasing the difference in length of each one. Try placing the blend off center. Try other methods of attaching the clasp.

Figure 14

Figure 15

Figure 16

THIS GORGEOUS PLANET

TROPICAL RAINFOREST

By including a clear, fresh aqua blue in the Hyacinth Macaw's cobalt, yellow, and black palette, Kristy Nijenkamp augments the playfulness of her lamp-worked beads.

From its floor to its strata of leafed canopies, the tropical rain forest offers up an eloquent and endless treasure trove of color inspiration. Struggling to receive what little sunlight reaches them, plants and animals on the ground adopt all kinds of strategies—and colors—to shape their lives. Look for palette polarities: gentle gradations and abrupt transitions, muted mergings and startling counterpoints, discreet protective coverings and gaudy color warnings.

Palm bark

149. Palm Bark

Nature is a supreme color sophisticate, and her finesse shows in this palette. Unfurling palm bark (left) in the rain forest reveals warm yellow-greens, soft pinkish-browns, and a streak or orange. Notice that DB-108 is a gold luster finished bead, furnishing a hint of purplish-pink.
Delicas: DB-371, DB-910, DB-108, DB-682

The vivid palette of the Rainbow Lorikeet, found in the rainforests of Australia, New Zealand, and Indonesia, inspired Margie Deeb's creation of dyed chalk turquoise and glass beads.

Heleconia

150. Heleconia Heaven

Heleconias are among the most beautiful and amazing flowers on the earth. This palette from the photo on the bottom left is tropical in every way. Go all out with the yellows and greens; place accents of orange and red with precision. The less red, the more attention-grabbing the result will be. **Delicas: DB-705, DB-274, DB-160, DB-1301, DB-703, DB-727**

151. Toucan

Like a tuxedo accessorized in bright costume jewelry, the playful toucan palette is full of contrast. Use it for casual jewelry, or fun, free-form sculptural pieces. **Delicas: DB-310, DB-201, DB-233, DB-651, DB-161, DB-165**

152. Rainforest Waterfall

From warm green leaves a waterfall spills into a cool, teal-colored lagoon deep within a Costa Rican rainforest. In this refreshing color scheme, the juxtaposition of warm and cool is bridged by white. Play up either the warm or cool shades and accent with pearly white. **Delicas: DB-776, DB-705, DB-274, DB-793, DB-078, DB-201**

Joan Babcock's micromacrame piece borrows colors and curves from the extraordinary pitcher plant, epenthes rafflesiana. These carnivores grow twelve-inch pitchers, which are usually chock full of digested insects. Cavandoli knotting, beads, and wire

Fruit Dove

153. Fruit Dove

The complementary pair of red and green form the basis for a charming color scheme based on a fruit dove (left), with small accents of buttercup yellow and bronze. **Delicas: DB-027, DB-203, DB-917, DB-914, DB-248, DB-233, DB-022**

154. Canopy Colors

The colors of the rainforest canopy find depth in darkened, cool greens, pizzazz in warm, yellow-greens, and strength in orange-tinted browns. The selected Delicas feature a variety of surface finishes—AB, matte, luster, and crystal-lined—to achieve a medley of textures. **Delicas: DB-027, DB-746, DB-877, DB-174, DB-170, DB-901**

155. Red-Eyed Tree Frog

Neon lime green is the dominant color of the red-eyed tree frog whose yellow lipstick, orange toes, and black eyeliner make a brilliant, exciting palette. **Delicas: DB-169, DB-161, DB-214, DB-010, DB-160**

156. Slipper Orchid

The Slipper Orchid of Borneo wears maroon and a range of curry-yellows that mingle, merge, and separate in a luxuriously exotic palette full of gradients. Wine colored striations and spots articulate the top of the bloom, adding leopard-like texture. **Delicas: DB-1312, DB-062, DB-1413, DB-781, DB-233**

Mediterranean blue-greens, oranges, and browns, like the hues in this Venetian skyline, coalesce in Heidi Kummli's embroidered *Dragonfly Necklace*.
Turquoise, glass, and metal beads on leather
Necklace photograph by Heidi Kummli

MEDITERRANEAN MAGIC

While Italy, Morocco, Spain, Turkey, France, and Croatia each have their own color dialects, they also share the waters of the Mediterranean Sea and its climate of wet winters and hot, dry summers. These sea-bordering areas yield soft, sun-drenched palettes strewn with brilliant floral accents, terracotta tiles, yellow and orange stucco, frosted grapes, jewel-blue waters, teal canals, and dusty olive-greens. Of the water itself, Vincent Van Gogh wrote, "The Mediterranean has the color of mackerel, changeable I mean. You don't always know if it is green or violet, you can't even say it's blue, because the next moment the changing reflection has taken on a tint of rose or gray." In the Iliad, Homer referred to it as the "wine dark sea." Like the color of ancient wine, the color that the poet had in mind is unclear, yet the poetic phrase evokes the sea's mystery and intoxication. When much debris and dust is in the air, the Mediterranean will seem to turn a deep red.

Shades of a Tuscan landscape inhabit Jamie Cloud Eakin's earrings of autumn jasper and glass seed beads.

Bright geraniums accent shades of green and terracotta

157. Tuscany

Brown and terracotta against a range of olive greens is the palette of the Tuscan hills (above). This near-complementary harmony explains part of it's the landscape's timeless appeal; sheer beauty must explain the rest. **Delicas: DB-027, DB-746, DB-877, DB-174, DB-170, DB-901**

158. Jolt of Geranium

Variation on a theme: geraniums (left) in full bloom surprise this classic terracotta/green harmony with their bright magenta-purple accents. **Delicas: DB-1302, DB-705, DB-877, DB-073, DB-214**

159. Camogli on the Italian Riviera

In the seaside village of Camogli the tall stacks of houses are brightly painted so the returning fishermen can recognize their home from offshore. Golden undertones and off-white trim unify the array of cheerful colors. **Delicas: DB-353, DB-742, DB-233, DB-235, DB-798, DB-729**

160. Spanish Window

The Moorish window (left) displays quite a spectrum of colors, beginning with an expanse of two distinct pastels. Tilework of stronger, more muted primary colors and green cover the surrounding wall. Its an odd juxtaposition of colors, but works well if you use the proportions similar to those in the photo. Use small quantities of the stronger tones. **Delicas: DB-1526, DB-206, DB-361, DB-098, DB-917, DB-651, DB-352**

Moorish style window

THIS GORGEOUS PLANET

Twilight Time
A palette of sparkling grape colors encircle SaraBeth Cullinan's glass and brass beaded bracelet.

Lake Kournas in Crete

Blue dome of Santorini

161. Lake Kournas

A cool, refreshing palette inspired by Crete's only natural, fresh-water lake exhibits an amazing range of blues and greens. The yellow-greens of plant life and a pale peach color, echoing tha of the soil, provide warmer accents. **Delicas: DB-714, DB-793, DB-861, DB-152, DB-353**

162. Mediterranean Blue I

This beautiful, stark, and simple palette arises from a familiar scene of Greek architecture overlooking the sea. The Delica line doesn't offer the exact shade of blue that covers stucco domes in Greece (left), but DB-730 will suffice, even though its undertones contain less green. **Delicas: DB-165, DB-730, DB-1490, DB-207**

163. The Olive Tree

A scene repeated all over Greece is the expanse of blue surrounding a wind-blown olive tree clinging to the dusty ground. Start with a matte blue for the sky (DB-861) and use three or more shades of yellow-greens. Cool, soft, muted green (DB-374) represents the distant hills. Accents of sandy-peach and deep, rich brown finish it off. **Delicas: DB-861, DB-371, DB-274, DB-910, DB-374, DB-353, DB-312**

164. Mediterranean Blue II

A refreshing palette of blues representing water, sky, and stucco domes of the Greek Isles. A cool palette often requires the injection of warmth to enliven the mood. But this one, which displays an abundance of sparkle and an AB finish, succeeds without introducing more color. **Delicas: DB-285, DB-861, DB-730, DB-1497, DB-1530**

THE AMERICAN SOUTHWEST

The American West and Southwest is a gift of towering stone sculptures, enormous skies, and brilliant light. All convey a sense of permanence and eternity. In this raw and rugged land of extremities, burnt orange plays a sovereign role. Juxtapose its warmth against sky blues and arid greens and you've formed the basis for palettes seen throughout New Mexico, Utah, and Colorado.

165. Arches

In Arches National Park, near Moab, Utah (left), millions of years of geologic history can be seen in layers of earth-orange strata. Blues complement the myriad browns, terracottas, and pumpkin shades of orange, creating a land of dazzling color contrasts. **Delicas: DB-760, DB-777, DB-287, DB-1497, DB-381, DB-1490**

Arches National Monument in Utah

A vintage Czech cabochon and amber colored butterflies made of Czech pressed glass bring to mind the blue, gold, and oranges of a sunset in Utah. Necklace by Jamie Cloud Eakin

The Colorado River winds through the Grand Canyon.

South Dakota Badlands

Antelope Canyon, Arizona

166. Grand Colors

An aerial view of the Colorado River winding through the Grand Canyon (left) inspired this variation on the red/green complementary harmony. The lighter colors are soft, producing an aged look. Green and red aventurine with moss agate accents recreate this scheme in stones. **Delicas: DB-327, DB-374, DB-372, DB-777, DB-1492, DB-1526, DB-311**

167. Badlands

This mineral palette inspired by South Dakota's Badlands (left) is built of low-intensity, complex tones. DB-911 and DB-103 bring a shimmer to the matte finishes. All of these colors can be found in jaspers and agates. **Delicas: DB-911, DB-374, DB-372, DB-103, DB-772, DB-731**

168. Blue Sky, Red Rock

Another variation of the staple palette of the Southwest. The blues have more green undertones than those of palette 165, and the oranges are slightly brighter, a bit less earthy. For the lighter blue, I used DB-057, an AB finish, to furnish even more color. **Delicas: DB-798, DB-1302, DB-057, DB-622**

169. Canyon Colors

As a darkened version of orange, brown adds depth and scope to this monochromatic scheme of deep oranges from the striated layers of a slot canyon (left). Working monochromatically is a great way to learn about value (lights and darks), and get to know a color up close and personal. **Delicas: DB-764, DB-773, DB-1363, DB-734, DB-1479**

In *Desert Dreams*, Kristy Nijenkamp mirrors a classic Arizona scene in glass beads. The dusty blue skies and the parched yellow-greens of the saguaro cactus are separated by clouds of textured ivory glass rolled in silver foil.

Mammoth Hot Springs

170. Mammoth Hot Springs

Microorganisms and living bacteria create beautiful shades of oranges, pinks, yellows, and greens in the hot springs at Yellowstone National Park (left). This unusual palette uses the cool blue-greens as the dominant, the off-white of deposited travertine as a unifying color, with accents of green and yellow from the surrounding plants. **Delicas: DB-729, DB-375, DB-211, DB-233, DB-908, DB-1454**

171. Amber Waves of Grain

These colors are those of the golden fields blanketing expanses of the heartland and the west. The blue of the sky makes a beautiful complement to honey tones and buttery yellows. **Delicas: DB-651, DB-742, DB-781, DB-233, DB-787, DB-861**

172. Painted Desert 2

The Painted Desert stretches southeast from the Grand Canyon to the Petrified Forest National Park. Covered by a very soft layer of mud, sandstone, and volcanic ash, the various minerals and decayed plant and animal matter fashion subtly contrasting ribbons of color across the land. **Delicas: DB-355, DB-354, DB-777, DB-353, DB-1526, DB-883, DB-1522**

THE LAY OF THE LAND

Leave the city and the land around you paints sweeping washes of color dotted with darks and lights. The earth furnishes so many ready-to-use palettes. When looking to landscapes, try to see the overall palette reduced to a few essential base colors—then look to details. The dark blue silk of a meandering river may be the final accent that rounds out a landscape palette of burnished yellows and greens.

The unusual colors of a Japanese maple tree surrounded by water, moss, and azaleas (above right) inspired Jamie Cloud Eakin to one of her finest creations. Cabs of ocean jasper, moukite, rhodonite, and rhyolite; pink coral, serpentine, rhodonite, and glass beads; patina metal leaves

A landscape of rich autumnal colors

Mountainscapes of the north are comprised of cool tones.

173. Autumn Scape

Grayed blues juxtaposed against intense, rich, autumnal tones drew me in to the photo at left. I've used grass green as the dominant force, but red or olive green (DB-663) would work equally well, and each would achieve a different look. Red intensifies the greens, and the overall effect is a palette of life-affirming vibrancy. **Delicas: DB-247, DB-371, DB-663, DB-764, DB-654, DB-377, DB-1451, DB-651, DB-233**

174. Mountain Lake

A range of soft blues plays the dominant role in this refreshing mountain lake scene (bottom left). Because the greens are the strongest colors, use them sparingly or they'll overpower other members of the palette. To keep it soft, accent with a dusting of white, and use the gentle gray (DB-381) as a unifying tone. **Delicas: DB-730, DB-381, DB-1405, DB-776, DB-1497, DB-746, DB-1490**

175. Sunset On the Coast

Any combination of blue and orange is compelling. Inspired by colors from a glowing coastal sunset scene, I've combined chalky, matte finished dusky blues with silky peaches. A hint of ceylon cream from frothy whitecaps lightens the mood. Call forth this understated yet powerful palette using peach moonstone or sunstone and denim lapis. **Delicas: DB-377, DB-376, DB-381, DB-684, DB-622, DB-203**

176. Quaking Aspens

Stands of quaking aspen trees stretch for miles in the Rocky Mountains. Alongside evergreens, their brilliant golden-yellow tones illuminate the landscape. Mix in as many shades of amber as you want. **Delicas: DB-160, DB-233, DB-651, DB-274, DB-705, DB-011, DB-653**

Cool Lava
Frieda Bates catches luminous auroral folds of color in her dichroic glass and braided strand. She rounds out the palette by adding yellow-greens and aqua blue.

CELESTIAL COMBINATIONS

Capturing the evanescent delicacy of light and color in the shifting sky is hardly possible using a physical medium. But that doesn't mean it's not worth trying! Tricks of temperature and particles create gauzy scarves of color best mimicked by using iridescent, transparent, and translucent bead finishes. Like the air palettes described on pages 14-15, aim for light-filled space and luminosity. Try to achieve not just the colors, but also the radiance and the changing mood of skyscapes.

The simultaneously blazing neons and pastels tints of sunset.

A deep space illustration of soft edges and dramatic hues.

An evening sky passion play

177. The Poetry of Sunset

Contrasts set this lyrical palette shimmering: warm and cool, saturated and muted. What you can't see in print are the surface finishes: each one is different. The sunset photo on the left is the inspiration, but I excluded the deep browns and blacks out of concern that they would turn this complex scheme into a confusing hodgepodge. **Delicas: DB-622, DB-764, DB-1413, DB-376, DB-233, DB-078, DB-1491**

178. Super Nova

Tempestuous and provocative, red simply won't be ignored. Pair it with black, and the duo creates a force to be reckoned with. Inspired by the deep space illustration on the left, I included hot magenta and then lightened the energy by adding a smooth buttercup yellow. The palette becomes striking and luxurious: a perfect color scheme for evening wear. **Delicas: DB-310, DB-159, DB-073, DB-233**

179. Passion in Pink and Purple

A spectacular range of purples and pinks are kept from becoming saccharin by touches of black and yellow. This gorgeous palette taken straight from the sky (left) is high drama and panache. **Delicas: DB-249, DB-1345, DB-245, DB-247, DB-661, DB-310, DB-233**

180. After the Storm

Darkened blue clouds of a dying storm are accented with a slightly muted pink (DB-072). One daring streak of bright pink (DB-914) slices through all the colors, bringing hope. **Delicas: DB-377, DB-361, DB-1405, DB-257, DB-072, DB-914**

Tuscan Headpin Earrings

Designed and created by SaraBeth Cullinan

BEGINNER

Instant jewelry-making gratification comes easy when you incorporate ready-made components into your design and color palette. Any color palette can be used for numerous of earring variations made on the simple foundation of headpins.

Inspired by an aerial view of Tuscany hills and rooftops, SaraBeth Cullinan creates five variations of simple, elegant earrings.

181. Tuscan Rooftops

An interpretation of the palette presented in the Tuscany photo (left), this project puts the focuses on the warm colors of the tiles and buildings. Accents of green in a matte silver-lined finish add depth, and a streak of blue-gray found in the sky cools it off like a fresh breeze. **Delicas: DB-777, DB-233, DB-322, DB-901, DB-287, DB-690, DB-381**

Materials
• one pair gold-filled 4mm ball and post earring findings
• one pair vermeil heart chandelier earring findings
• twelve gold-filled head 2" headpins (.020 or .022 diameter) ¹/₂ hard
• ten 3mm bicone crystals, Indian red
• ten 3mm bicone crystals, jet
• ten 3mm pearls, powder almond
• ten 4mm bicone crystals, Indian sapphire
• ten 4mm pearls, copper
• ten 4mm bicone crystals, dark tourmaline
• ten 4mm pearls, brown
• twelve 4mm bicone crystals, Indian red

Tools
• forty-four size 80 seed beads, matte metallic bronze
• wire nipper
• chain-nosed pliers

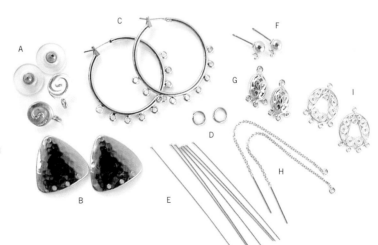

A. Decorative earring posts and backs. B. 3-hole hammered gold-plated triangles. C. 9-hole hoops. D. Jumprings. E. 2" .020 gold-filled ¹/₂ hard headpins. F. 4mm ball post earring findings. G. 3-hole mini-chandelier earring components. H. 4" ear threads. I. 4-hole round filigree chandelier earring components.

Heart Chandelier Earrings

These directions are for the Heart Chandelier Earrings. To make headpin dangles, see directions below.

Center loop of heart chandelier

On a headpin, place one Indian red 4mm bicone. Make loop and attach to the chandelier component.

Headpin dangles

On a 2" headpin stack on one each of:

indian red 4mm crystal
brown 4mm pearl
dark tourmaline 4mm crystal
copper 4mm pearl
Indian sapphire 4mm crystal
powder almond 3mm pearl
jet 3mm crystal
Indian red 3mm crystal

Repeat for a total of ten head pins and attach to the chandelier. Attach chandelier to the ball and post earring findings.

4" Ear Thread with Vermeil Chandelier Component

All headpin dangles are the same length. One 3.2mm 20GA jump ring is used to connect the vermeil component to the ear thread. When making earrings with ear thread, keep them light in weight so they don't slide out of the earlobe. When wearing, slide a clear rubber earring stopper behind the lobe on each thread to assure that they'll hang the same length.

Hammered Gold-plated Triangles with Decorative Vermeil Posts

Use one 3.2mm 20GA jump ring for every headpin, and two jump rings to connect to each post. The center headpin has two extra beads on it to make it the longest dangle.

Vermeil Round Filigree Chandelier on 4mm Vermeil Posts

The center two headpins have two extra beads on them to make them the longest dangles.

9-Hole Vermeil Hoops

Hoop earrings use one 3.2mm 20GA jump ring for every headpin. Each hoop has six short headpin dangles, and three long headpin dangles.

Crystal & Lampwork Pendant

Designed and created by Kristy Nijenkamp

INTERMEDIATE

Using an artisan lampwork bead as a focal point, string aurora borealis colors into intricate swags dotted with silver stars.

Celestial Swirls
Kristy Nijenkamp creates an Aurora Borealis in her original lampworked bead and crystal necklace.

182. Aurora Borealis

The greens in this aurora borealis photo make liquid-smooth gradations; undertones shift from blue to yellow, while value shifts from dark to light. These sublime and subtle color movements are heightened by tiny accents of black and the palest mint. Jade, chalcedonies and aventurines with onyx accents work with this scheme. **Delicas: DB-788, DB-918, DB-759, DB-237, DB-1536, DB-301**

FINISHED LENGTH: 22"

Materials
- .014 Softflex beading wire (fine)
- 8mm -10mm silver bail
- One 21 gauge .028" sterling silver, headpin
- two 3mm size .082 sterling silver crimp beads, center hole
- one 6mm x 4mm sterling saucer beads
- four sterling silver spacer beads
- sterling silver clasp
- (151) 4mm teal crystal bicones
- (121) 4mm sapphire crystal bicones

- thirteen 6mm crystal bicones, sapphire
- six 8mm crystal bicones, teal
- forty-seven 2mm sterling silver round beads

Tools
- round-nosed pliers
- wire nipper
- chain-nosed pliers
- crimping pliers

Pendant

On headpin stack one 6mm sapphire crystal bicone, the focal lampworked bead, one sterling saucer bead, one 4mm teal crystal bicone, and one 2mm sterling round. (The 6mm bicone and saucer bead will stabilize the lampworked bead and become partially obscured by it.) Make a wire loop with the rest of the headpin and finish as shown on page 170. Hang the headpin from the bail. Close bail with pliers if necessary.

Teal Foundation Strand

Cut three 24" pieces of Softflex and temporarily tape one end, leaving at least a 3" tail, to keep beads from sliding off. As your stringing tip becomes frayed, clip it to make it sharp again (the specified length allows four extra inches for clipping).

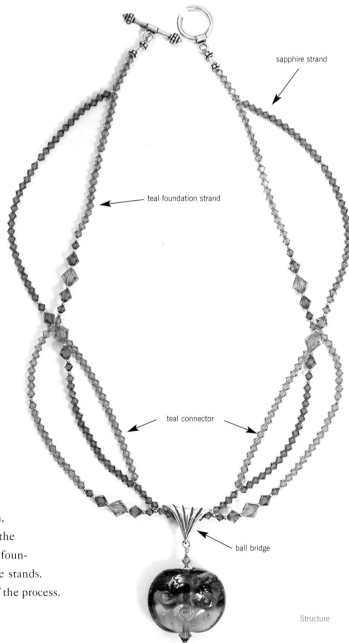

sapphire strand

teal foundation strand

teal connector

ball bridge

Structure

String on:

thirteen teal 4mm bicones
one sterling round
eleven teal 4mm bicones

Sequence A:

one sterling round
one sapphire 4mm bicone
one sterling round
one sapphire 6mm bicone
one sterling round
one teal 8mm bicone
one sterling round
one sapphire 6mm bicone

one sterling round
one sapphire 4mm bicone
eleven teal 4mm bicones
one sterling round
thirteen teal 4mm bicones
Sequence A
one sterling round
seven teal 4mm bicones

These even teal bicones will be referred to as the "bail bridge." Slide your bail and pendant over the bail bridge now and continue stringing a mirror image of the beads you just strung, working backwards up the stringing pattern, from bottom to top. Temporarily tape the end of the wire close to the last teal bicone. This will be your foundation strand upon which you will build two more stands. You will not crimp any strands until the very end of the process.

Sapphire Strand

Pull one of the cut pieces of Softflex through the first five teal bicones of the foundation strand and leave a tail the same length as the tail of the foundation strand. Temporarily tape this end.

Bring strand to the outside of the necklace and string on:

one sterling round
thirteen sapphire 4mm bicones
one sterling round
nineteen sapphire 4mm bicones
sterling round
twenty-one sapphire 4mm bicones

Pass beading wire through the bail bridge. Continue strand by stringing a mirror image of the beads you just strung, working backwards up the stringing pattern, from bottom to top. Pass beading wire through the last five teal bicones of the foundation strand and temporarily tape the tail end close to the last teal bicone.

Teal Connector

Pull the third piece of Softflex through the foundation strand and exit at the end of Sequence A. Leave a tail the same length as the tail of the foundation strand. Temporarily tape this end.

Make sure the sapphire strand is underneath the foundation strand.

Look at the three-strand intersection photo, and you'll see that the 8mm teal bicone holds all three strands together, even though only two strands pass through it.

Lay the wire of the connector strand over and in between the sterling round of the sapphire strand. Pass through the 8mm teal bicone. String on:

twenty teal 4mm bicones
one sterling round

Pass through four sapphire 4mm bicones of the sapphire strand then through the bail bridge. Continue the connector strand by stringing a mirror image of the beads you just strung. Exit through the last five teal bicones of the foundation strand and temporarily tape the tail end close to the last teal bicone.

Untape all ends and pull all strands snug, especially at the intersection point. Slip a spacer, a crimp, and a spacer over each bunch of three strands at each end. Attach to clasp and finish as shown on page 171. Slide the wires through as many teal bicones as possible before snipping.

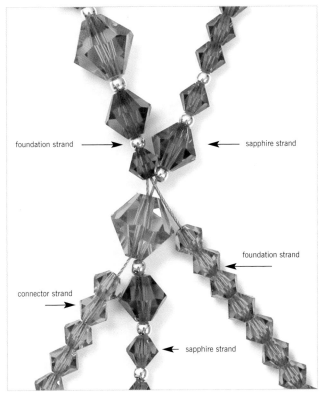

foundation strand

sapphire strand

foundation strand

connector strand

sapphire strand

3-strand intersection (not yet tightened)

Rainforest Cascade Necklace

Designed and created by Margie Deeb

INTERMEDIATE

> Many strands of carefully selected beads varying slightly in size spill from a twisted multi-strand collar.

183. Orchid in the Rainforest

A surprisingly easy palette to work with. Use far less of the magenta tones than the greens, letting them serve as accents, as in the rainforest photo. This is one of nature's more spectacular harmonies. **Delicas: DB-776, DB-754, DB-917, DB-1414, DB-073, DB-247, DB-281**

FINISHED LENGTH: 32"

Materials
- 20 gms size 11o seed beads in at least six shades of greens
- 10 gms size 11o seed beads in at least three shades of magenta
- 2 gms size 14o beads, green
- 5 gms size 6o and/or 8o seed beads, green
- 5gms size 6o and/or 8o seed beads, magenta
- twenty-four brass leaves, green patina
- eighteen brass leaves, magenta patina
- size 11 looming needle (extra long)

- size 12 beading needle
- Size D Nymo thread, green; dark pink
- two 4" vermeil headpins
- vermeil cones
- vermeil clasp

Tools
- drafting tape
- blunt-end tweezers

Foundation

Using an extra long looming needle, string 15 1/2" of green beads onto a 23" length of Nymo D green thread. Center the beads on the thread, leaving 3 1/2" to 4" of thread on either side of the beads. Make twenty-seven strands. The easiest way to accomplish this tedious task is to secure a measuring tape to your table or board, and tape down each strand (both ends) as you create them. Tie a knot on one end of the strand, tape it down with the edge of the tape against the knot, and string your beads. Do not tie the other end yet. You may need to add or remove a few beads in the future. I use white drafting tape because it is easily removable and leaves no residue. Make sure the length of strung beads on each strand is exactly the same. To allow for a better fit inside the cones, thread the last 1/4" to 3/4" of each end of each strand with size 14o green beads (figure 1.)

As you string, pepper each strand with accents of 6o and 11o green beads, different shades of green 11o beads, and a couple magenta 8o or 6o beads.

Margie Deeb uses lush texture and vivid complementary colors to create the excitement of these brilliant orchids in a Singapore rainforest.

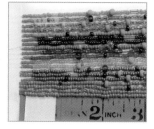
Figure 1

When all strands are complete, tie off the open end of each strand by tying two or three strands together (at one end only) with one overhand knot. Be sure to close any gaps so there is no visible thread showing in the strand before you tie off.

Now tie three groups of four, and three groups of five strands together on one end with an overhand knot, taking great care to keep all tail threads bunched evenly together. Wetting the threads helps (I dip the ends into a small cup of water). Tie all the thread tails of the other end together in the same way. Split the bunch of tails in half (figure 2) and finish each end with a cone as shown on page 171. Add a 6o bead onto the wire before making the loop (figure 3.) Add clasp. Twist the whole bunch of strands a couple of times and you are finished with the foundation.

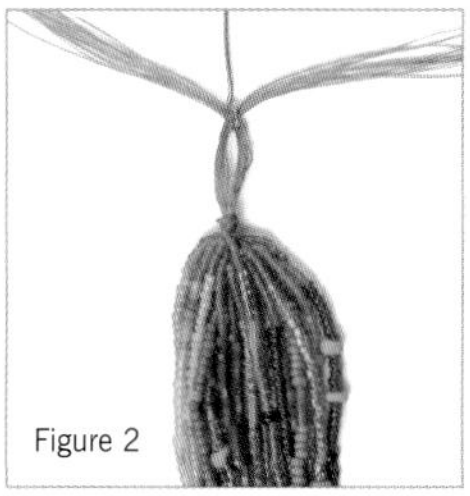

Cascade

Thread needle with 36" of Nymo. Make a 21-stack/3-deep brick stitch ladder (see page 176). If you are using size 6o seed beads, make a 2-drop stack. If you are using size 6o seed beads, make a 3-drop stack. I used both: size 6o green beads and size 8o magenta beads. You'll see that the height of two 6o beads equals the height of three 8o beads. Use the color pattern shown in Figures 4 and 4a. Fold the ladder in half so ten stacks are centered in front of eleven stacks. The ten stacks are the front. Sew together as shown in figure 5.

Figure 2

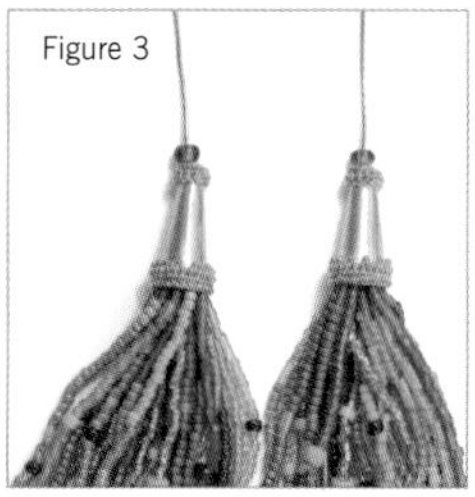

Figure 3

Figure 4

Figure 4a

Figure 5

Back row: 11 stacks

Front row: 10 stacks

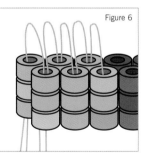

Figure 6

Make twenty-seven beaded loops arranged from front to back as shown in figure 6. Those closest to the ends should be 3 3/8" long. Reduce the length of the loops as you work toward the center to accommodate for the curve of the foundation. The center four loops should be 3" long. Measure each loop carefully before sewing it into the beads.

Make forty-two fringe (two exiting each stack of the ladder). It's not necessary to make each loop correspond with a fringe. Tie small knots along the ladder threads (figure 3) after each loop and fringe. This insures that if a strand breaks, the wearer will lose only the beads from that strand.

I made the fringe graduate light to dark from the outside in and short to long (with a few exceptions so it looked more organic). I also made a few short fringe in the center of the magenta area so magenta leaves would be visible all the way down the cascade. Measured from the bottom of the ladder to the tip of the leaf, make the shortest fringe 3 1/2", and the longest 9 1/2". Stop from time to time and slide a bead tube through the loops and let the cascade hang. Don't aim for perfect symmetry—this is the rainforest we're emulating (figure 7). Make the fringe lush and textural.

When all fringe is complete, slide a bead tube through the loops to open them (figure 7a). Using blunt nosed tweezers, gently pull the foundation through the loops as you ease the tube out. Use the tweezers to arrange the loops correctly on the foundation.

Figure 7a

Figure 7

Lavender Rose Brooch

Designed and created by Thom Atkins

ADVANCED

Dichroic glass cabochons set in bead bezels are the center of this peyote-stitched rose. Thom Atkins' meticulous details reflect the dusty colors of the yewbarrow and wastwater in the United Kingdom's Lake District.

> Use advanced peyote stitch skills and cabochons to weave a quietly elegant rose brooch of texture and intrigue.

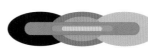

184. Heathered Moors

Nature has outdone herself with this complex arrangement of unusual hues. The proportions here establish the mauve-violets as the dominant tones, but you could just as easily make greens the main force and accent with the violet tones. The earth orange serves the palette best as an accent color. **Delicas: DB-923, DB-799, DB-629, DB-381, DB-777, DB-371, DB-910**

Materials
- size 14o and size 11o seed beads, mix of greens, browns, mauve, lavender
- fifteen to twenty 2mm and 3mm round beads (to match colors as shown)
- one dichroic cabochon 1¹/₂" diameter (to match colors as shown)
- three small ¹/₂" round dichroic cabochons (to match colors as shown)
- size 11 harp needle
- Size D Nymo D thread in appropriate colors
- Terrifically Tacky Tape (or comparable double-sided craft tape)
- Ultrasuede for backing, four to six square inches
- 1¹/₂" long brooch pin
- pattern plastic, four to six square inches (available in most fabric and quilt stores)

Bezeled Cabochons

Cut a loose oval-shaped piece of Ultrasuede the size you want your finished brooch to be. Apply Terrifically Tacky Tape to the back of the cabochon, trim the edges, and attach it to the center of the Ultrasuede base.

You will be using the backstitch to attach seed beads to the Ultrasuede. Thread a size 11 sharp needle with Nymo D thread. If the beads you are using vary in size, set the thinnest aside and use the thickest beads for this first row. Thread a knot on one end of 1 yard of Nymo thread; thread a needle on the other end. Push the needle up through the back of the suede, exiting right next to the cabochon. Add four size 11o seed beads, place them next to the stone so they lay snug but not bunched up. Push your needle back down through the suede right next to the last bead you threaded. Bring needle back up between the second and third bead, as close to the cabochon as possible, and pass through beads 3 and 4. Add four more beads. Repeat until you have circled the whole stone with an even number of beads. If necessary, adjust the number of beads at the end by adding or subtracting one or two. Thread back through the whole row to tighten the beads against the cabochon.

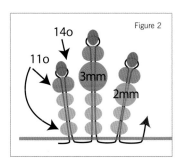

Figure 1

Pass needle through the first bead in the circle and add a bead onto the thread. Skip a bead in the existing row and pass needle through the next. Do this all the way around the cabochon, pulling the thread snug (figure 1).

Pass through the last bead in the bottom row, come up, and pass through the first bead in the second row. Add a bead, and pass through the next bead in that row, adding a bead after you pass through a bead. Continue on around the cab. Depending on the shape of the cabochon you may want to use the thin beads you set aside for this third row. You'll probably want to create another row or two of the size 11o beads before adding two last rows of the smaller, size 14o beads, which will pull in the top of the bezel.

When your bezel is far enough over the rim of the cabochon to hold it in place, and you've added at least two rows of size 14o beads, pull the thread tight. If the holes in the bead will allow, pass through the last two rows again for reinforcement. (These last two rows will appear to be one row.) This helps snug the beads tightly against the cabochon. After reinforcing the last two rows as many times as possible, work your way through the beads back down through the suede to the back, knot and clip off the tail of the thread.

Figure 2

14o

11o

3mm

2mm

Follow the same attaching procedure and bezel around the 3 small round cabochons.

Make flower stamens all around the bezeled cabochon. Sew stacks of 11o beads topped by either an 11o, 2mm, or a 3mm bead and a terminating 14o bead (figure 2).

Petals

The petals are created individually using the peyote stitch in freeform style—make them up as you go! (See pages 172–173 for peyote instructions.) Each petal begins with a row of backstitch (use the darkest color of beads) the width of the base of the petal stitched to the Ultrasuede. Increase at the ends and in the middle of each row so the petal "grows" out and up. If you want the curve to go straight up, don't increase in the center. Use lighter colored beads as you reach the outer edges of each petal.

When you've reached the desired width and curve, begin decreasing both the ends and the center. If you want a slight ruffle effect at the top of the petal, increase a lot. More increasing equals more ruffle (figure 3). The number of petals you want will depend on the size and shape of your cabochon. I made an initial row of four, then backstitched more rows behind and overlapping these, for a total of eight petals.

Figure 3

Backing

When you've finished all bezeled cabs, stamens, and petals, back-stitch a final row of beads around all beadwork. Trim the Ultrasuede within a 1/16", apply pattern plastic (cut slightly smaller), pin back, and a back of Ultrasuede (cut slightly larger). (Figure 4.) Trim front and back suede against the edge of this final row. Now you will do a simple beaded blanket stitch around the edge of the entire piece, which will simultaneously sandwich all layers together and finish the edge. With a doubled knotted thread bring the needle up through the front face between two beads. Pass through one bead. Go out around both edges and come up from the back beyond the bead you just passed through. Go through the next bead, out around both edges, etc. until you have worked your way all the way around the edge of the brooch. You'll attach the leaves to this row of blanket stitched beads.

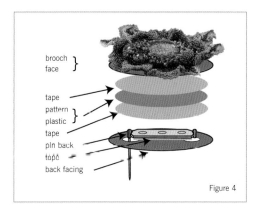

Figure 4

brooch
face }
tape
pattern
plastic }
tape
pin back
tape
back facing

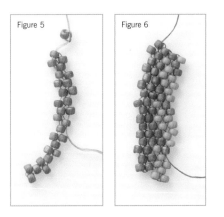

Figure 5

Figure 6

Leaves

Use 14o beads in free-form peyote to create each leaf. Stitch them to the edge of the brooch backing, right up against the petals. Secure them to the back of the petals as well.

Begin each leaf by creating a center vein, as long as you want the leaf to be, using your darkest leaf color. Using straight peyote stitch, decrease with each row at the tip of the leaf, working one side at a time (figures 5 and 6). Make two vein rows, one on each side of the base row. Using leaf colors peppered with the vein color (to suggest branching veins), build outward, increasing within the row every third or fourth bead. As with the petals, a wavy edge is created by increasing more as you move further away from the center vein.

To finish the leaf, add a raised vein row down the center of size 11o beads in the vein color at the base, tapering down to smaller beads at the tip (figure 7). Attach leaves to the final row of beads surrounding the brooch (figure 8).

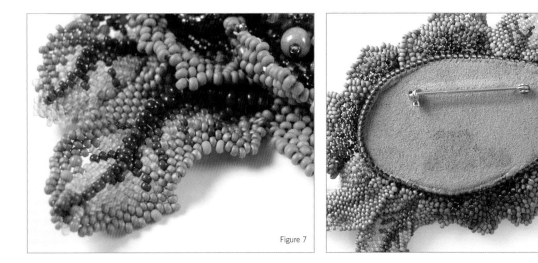

Figure 7

Figure 8

LIVING COLOR

CREEPING, CRAWLING COLOR

Gently muted yellow-green sparked with gold reflects a moth's delicate palette in Margie Deeb's peridot, vermeil, and glass multi-strand necklace.

Talk about palettes—the study of dragonfly colors alone could occupy a lifetime. This empire is second only to flowers in its diversity of astounding color schemes.

Orient yourself to look closely; pay deep attention to their world of minute spaces. It is a world of color spasms—iridescent jeweled butterflies and muted monochromatic moths, fashionably chic ladybugs and costumed caterpillars. And all their colors harmonize beautifully with shades of green.

If you didn't see it, you wouldn't believe it—clownish colors on grasshoppers! Carol Cypher exchanges yellow-orange for yellow, and pushes the blue towards green. She echoes their patterned intricacy by wrapping black and white "antennae" around the entire bracelet.
African helix stitch with glass seed beads

Oranges and reds hover over a host of greens. Glass and handmade polymer clay beads designed and contsructed by Carol Zilliacus.

Attacus Atlas Moth

Fashion forward moth

One bold bug pairs vivid primary colors with black

185. Attacus Atlas Moth

Found only in Southeast Asia, this stunning creature is called the Atlas Moth (left). Its patterns resemble maps and display triangular transparent "windows." In our complex palette, they are colored a soft aloe-green, a striking complement to the dominant reds. **Delicas: DB-654, DB-280, DB-922, DB-1414, DB-233, DB-310, DB-1491**

186. Moth Magic

This fashion conscious moth (left) must be the belle of the ball, wearing an enchanting green on black ensemble topped off with a splash of red. Try this in hematite, jades or malachite, and a touch of carnelian or garnet. Play up the contrasts. Go as bright as you dare with the greens. **Delicas: DB-310, DB-237, DB-1536, DB-727**

187. Yellow Blue Bug

A classic blue and yellow duet (bottom left) is filled out and enlivened by the addition of vivid yellow-greens. Accents of black turn them into a playful, bold, casual scheme based on the brightly colored bug and its leaf. **Delicas: DB-165, DB-688, DB-174, DB-160, DB-010**

188. Dream of the Damselfly

A damselfly of shimmering aqua blue and orange on a lime-green leaf inspired a palette fit for a tropical cruise. AB finishes against matte beads deliver more sparkle than they do on their own, and the contrast of the two creates depth. In gemstones, use turquoise, carnelian, and peridot. **Delicas: DB-166, DB-078, DB-744, DB-169**

Lime green butterfly on orange

Classic butterfly blues

189. Effervescence

You have to see the actual beads to experience the shimmering light of this exquisite palette. Based on the photo of the lime-green butterfly (above), these delicate high notes work together to create an enchanting magic. Use the darkest color, DB-172, sparingly to add depth.
Delicas: DB-151, DB-752, DB-174, DB-860, DB-245, DB-248, DB-172

190. Butterfly Blues

The photo of the blue and orange butterfly above was the springboard for this scheme, but I've veered from its vividness, making the hues, contrasts, and transitions gentler. Rather than stark black I've included a charcoal grey. All colors are slightly muted, and the green and orange are much cooler. The palette retains its bold complementary harmony, yet is more sophisticated and complex. **Delicas: DB-165, DB-760, DB-917, DB-301, DB-235, DB-1490**

191. Catchy Caterpillar Colors

The playful colors of the Black Swallowtail Butterfly Caterpillar are interpreted in beads using opaque AB finishes and a matte black. Bright yellow-green is the dominant force; black and orange are minute but startling accents. Switch the dominant color for a completely different effect. **Delicas: DB-169, DB-310, DB-161**

192. Anthera Polyphemus

In a palette as gentle as a moth, amber, gray, and mauve converge into thoughtful companions. I would never have dreamed these hues could work together so beautifully. It was the Anthera Polyphemus moth that showed me this elegant scheme. Include citrine or amber, rose quartz, and hematite. **Delicas: DB-651, DB-233, DB-749, DB-210, DB-001, DB-800**

The palette of *Painted Rock*, by Rebecca Thompson Brown, is that of the adult Map Butterfly (below) and its surroundings, with the surprise element of muted violets and lavender. Bead embroidery and peyote stitch. Glass beads, rock from Namibia.

LIVING COLOR

THE BRINY DEEP

With an orange and hot pink scarab, Jamie Cloud Eakin gives a nod to the Tropical Squarespot fish. She adds purple and exchanges the fish's bright yellow for gold, making the scheme more palatable for jewelry. Yellow works fine for the fish, gold works better for the humans. Bead embroidery and edging

Poet Mary Oliver writes of the ocean, "This enormity, this cauldron of changing greens and blues, is the great palace of the earth."

A dazzling array of hues lurk beneath the ocean's surface, many of which we may never see. Someone with an outrageous sense of color concocted this vast realm of pastels, muted shades, vibrants, and jewel tones that sway and swim in the currents. Flash photography allows us to perceive a sea creature's true colors untinted by the veil of water through which we view it with naked eyes.

Wrasse fish

193. Wrasse

Wrasse (left) are among the most colorful fish on the planet. More than 600 species sport an amazing range of extraordinary palettes, this being one of the more tame ones! Black makes a lively accent, taking the blue-to-green analogous scheme from an evocative oceanic palette to a chic color combination perfect for high fashion. **Delicas: DB-215, DB-793, DB-787, DB-724, DB-010**

Kristy Nijenkamp's lampworked bead emulates the colors and movement of the red lionfish underwater.
Necklace by Margie Deeb

Copperband Butterflyfish

Parrot Fish

194. Copperband Butterflyfish

I've rendered the Copperband Butterfly's bold color scheme (left) in highly reflective and AB surface finishes. Flashes of pink and hints of green furnish more color than exists in the original palette. The overall effect is one of striking color and magical texture. **Delicas: DB-160, DB-201, DB-063, DB-167, DB-001**

195. Parrotfish

Shimmering blue and teal act as a background for flashing, neon-like accents colors in this festive, parrotfish palette of pure scintillation (left). **Delicas: DB-178, DB-918, DB-1340, DB-160, DB-161, DB-010**

196. Anemone

Attached to a bed of coral, a reef anemone undulates with the currents. Its many tendril-like arms transition in color from creamy off-white, to pink, to electric purple. A dazzlingly simple combination with so much potential. **Delicas: DB-1491, DB-352, DB-247, DB-1345**

Carol Zilliacus captures the gentle radiance of sun in the colors of shells and starfish. Glass and hand made polymer clay beads designed and contructed by Carol Zilliacus.

THE SEA SHORE

If sunbleached, sandwashed colors make you swoon, the seashore may be your greatest source of inspiration. From soft yellows and oranges to pinks, beiges, and lavenders, the warmth of the sun kisses these palettes with golden undertones. Myriad browns and grays become low-intensity partners to pastel shell tints. Spots of bright colors make an appearance, like a crab shell as orange as candy. Gold findings and clasps add the final touch.

Sea turtle

197. Sea Turtle

A troupe of sandy shoreline tones cover the sea turtle (left). Since they are both analogous and similar in value, you can be quite flexible with proportions of each. Plan very carefully for the blue and black, however, placing small amounts of them exactly where you want to focus attention. **Delicas:** DB-1302, DB-901, DB-1451, DB-1478, DB-233, DB-218, DB-310

Glass pearls of varying shapes and sizes furnish the warm luster and organic nature of the shoreline palette.
Necklace and earring set by Margie Deeb

Chambered nautilus shell

Crab in the sand

198. Nautilus

The inner chambers of the nautilus shell (left) spiral from ivory tones into mysterious shades of purple-blue. In the bead palette, the lightest and darkest colors are AB finishes, which give a shell-like, iridescent glow. **Delicas: DB-157, DB-205, DB-1457, DB-381, DB-377, DB-799, DB-059**

199. Crab in the Sand

I've used the entire photograph on the top left for this palette, rendering the warm colors of the crab, the cool shadows on the sand in the late afternoon, and the surrounding shells. The warm/cool juxtaposition creates subtle tension, thus a livelier palette. **Delicas: DB-376, DB-381, DB-1456, DB-203, DB-101, DB-915, DB-734**

200. Urchin Sophisticate

A tropical sea urchin gives us a gentle, sandy-beige and mauve harmony which conveys a classic, elegant look perfect for mother-of-pearl, wooden agate, and amethyst. Or try this in bone and shell—many heishi come in these exact shades. **Delicas: DB-629, DB-695, DB-069, DB-203**

THE BLOOMING WORLD

Oh, the astounding come-hither colors of flowers—the abundant inspiration never ends! While stalking palettes based on florals, look at both the big picture—the entire garden itself—and the close-up—one solo blossom. Watch for the color shifts in the peculiarities of a single petal. Blossoms like orchids secrete tiny pockets of surprise color. If you tend to bright and vibrant palettes, exotic tropicals, like heleconias and gingers, deliver dazzling colors.

Norah's Whimsical Reticule
Margo Field consulted with a passion flower for this unusual palette.
Peyote stitch and netting mimic the flower's mandala.
Glass pearls, beads, and Swarovski rivoli cabochons

Fluffy Donuts
A fantasy-inspired bouquet of analogous colors designed by Rebekah Wills and created by Frieda Bates.
Petal, flower, and leaf-shaped pressed glass built over gemstone donuts

Living Lava Necklace
Elizabeth Ann Scarborough pushed the colors of a plumeria blossom into high gear by intensifying and saturating them to the extreme.
Dichroic cab by Patti Eastman
Bead embroidery and helix stitch

Majestic yellow orchids

Violet and green, a perennial combination

201. Elegance

Pairing two sunny shades of yellow-orange with more mature versions of crimson and raspberry makes this magnificent orchid's palette (left) both vivacious and sophisticated. Though part of the natural color scheme, the splash of green is delightfully surprising when taken out of context. **Delicas: DB-233, DB-742, DB-062, DB-1312, DB-705**

202. Cool Passion

Violet (or purple) and green work beautifully together in almost any version (think of amethyst and malachite, or amethyst and peridot). In this scheme both violet and green are very cool with blue undertones. The white and fuchsia accents create an arresting focal point, as they do in the flower on the left. **Delicas: DB-661, DB-919, DB-1530, DB-1345**

203. Orchid Drama

An orchid of breathtaking color prompted this trio. How can three colors radiate such beauty and energy? The secret is in the near-complementary relationship. Marry purple (or a purple that leans toward magenta, like these do) to yellow and you've got a color union that will rivet anyone's attention. **Delicas: DB-074, DB-233, DB-1345**

204. Off the Garden Wall

Another spectacular orchid scheme plucked straight from the garden (and enhanced by my sensibilities). Candy pink flirts shamelessly with brilliant lime-green (and a sparkling AB finish). Paired as such, these colors demand immediate, undivided attention. **Delicas: DB-174, DB-169, DB-247**

LIVING COLOR

Galaxy
Crimson and green in its many variations is a perpetual favorite. Frieda Bates mingles flashes of gold (cut beads) in place of the Cymbidium Orchid's yellow.
Herringbone stitch and bead embroidery
Dichroic glass by Frieda Bates
Necklace photograph by Haigwood Studios

Columbine blossom

Bougainvillea

Pansy

205. Columbine

Muted, soft pink of the columbine (left) sets the tone. The white acts as a counterpoint, bringing light and space into the scheme. Inspired by the ladybug, I threw in a jolt of red (omitting the black because it's too heavy for this palette). **Delicas: DB-800, DB-210, DB-1490, DB-854, DB-374, DB-098**

206. Bougainvillea

Behold the bougainvillea (left), a visual tumult of sense-pounding color! These radiant analogous blooms are hotter than hot! For accents I've used a soft yellow rather than white as nature has done in the tiny florets. This is less stark, and may be preferable in a piece of jewelry. Try white if you like. **Delicas: DB-161, DB-073, DB-159, DB-1491**

207. Pansy

A solid complementary relationship, violet and yellow, makes such an alluring color scheme little else is needed. The pansy (bottom left) uses white accents. Two shades of purple enhance the intensity of the contrast and provide textural interest because the surfaces finishes are different from one another. **Delicas: DB-610, DB-661, DB-160, DB-201**

208. Heavenly Hues of the Hibiscus

An array of pinks, some warm with orange leanings, some with cool with purple leanings, work with yellow and a dash of chartreuse to recreate the hues of a hibiscus. **Delicas: DB-914, DB-236, DB-1371, DB-244, DB-778, DB-233, DB-174**

Peacock Nouveau Set
Modulated color and form, yet still recognizable as peacock inspired, Elizabeth Ann Scarborough's embroidered dichroic glass necklace combines harmonious cools with gold accents.

FEATHERED FRIENDS

Winged creatures who soar so close to the realm where gods and goddesses roam, birds mesmerize us. They open our minds to lofty dreams. Let them also inspire our palettes to take flight.

The flare of a red-winged blackbird's epaulets, the feathery shifts from grey to white of the barn owl, the glide from pale to fervent coral of the flamingo, birds present a flock of ways to move from one color to the next.

Rose-ringed parakeets

Great horned owl

209. Rose-ringed Parakeets

The delightful colors of these rose-ringed parakeet siblings peeping out of their tree-nest hole (above) inspired an array of yellow-greens highlighted with bold accents. Do as the birds do: use only a hint of yellow, black, and white. **Delicas: DB-690, DB-163, DB-910, DB-169, DB-295, DB-233, DB-203, DB-001**

210. Great Horned Owl

In the distinct palette of the great horned owl (above), warm neutrals form a bridge between black and ivory. A luminous spark of yellow injects energy. Transitions among the browns and beiges should be gentle, like feathers. Black and ivory can punctuate, outline, frame, and/or accent. This palette is ready-made for jaspers, agates, hematite, and sparks of citrine or amber. **Delicas: DB-764, DB-901, DB-1456, DB-010, DB-233, DB-352**

211. The Rooster Crows

Like the owl palette above, black, ivory, and neutrals accented with a bright tone form an elegant, vivacious color scheme. Richness and depth are gained by deep teal (DB-919). Red struts about with head-turning flair in this rooster-inspired palette. Red coral among hematite, malachite, tiger-eye, and mother-of-pearl would carry this out in gemstones. **Delicas: DB-310, DB-301, DB-919, DB-272, DB-742, DB-203, DB-654, DB-757**

212. Flamingo

I couldn't resist the mostly monochromatic palette of the flamingo. Its coral-pink tones shifting from dark to light are so charming. The dash of black keeps it from saccharin sweetness. The allure of peach moonstone is similar to that of the flamingo's color. **Delicas: DB-070, DB-207, DB-1532, DB-1520, DB-001**

Robin Atkins borrowed colors from the Emperor penguin's ensemble, as well as the graceful shape from the curving arc of its head and neck. Bead embroidered pin

These palettes declare, "don't you dare!" What seems like decoration or panache is pure utility. Creatures of all species display excessively showy hues and combinations for protection—and would-be predators back off. Sometimes, those wearing these flashy warning signs aren't poisonous or venomous at all. They know that the empty threat of just wearing the colors is enough to keep them safe.

Use these palettes to startle and delight rather than to scare your viewers away. They are guaranteed attention-grabbers.

The poisonous dart frog of lowland rainforests employs a fashionable combination of teal and black to attract attention, as Margie Deeb did in her glass, multi-strand necklace.

Bamboo viper

Digitalis

213. Bamboo Viper

This is one gorgeous snake! Keep the palette as simple as the serpent's: three colors, two of them brilliant. The chartreuse and yellow are transparent beads with AB finishes, but you could use opaque AB finishes to a similar effect. Try this without the white—it's even more malevolent! **Delicas: DB-174, DB-053, DB-066**

214. Witches' Gloves

Depending on the species, digitalis may contain deadly toxins. Thus its sinister nicknames of Dead Man's Bells and Witches' Gloves. We get this stunning palette from the photo of the *Digitalis purpurea* (left) and its background greens. Three shades of purple and magenta represent the purple. The green is taken from the Bamboo Viper palette above—a transparent AB finish. Off-white Ceylon is less stark than bright white. **Delicas: DB-1345, DB-247, DB-074, DB-174, DB-1530**

Mary Hicklin reinterprets a poisonous dart frog's palette using the darker blue of lapis, coral, and an incised lapis frog inset with coral and turquoise by Pete Natewa. Necklace photograph by Melinda Holden.

Poison arrow frog

215. So Cute, but Not So Cuddly

Found in the rain forests of Central and South America, tiny Poison Arrow frogs wear astonishing color schemes. Some expose a flash of yet another bright hue when they jump. Their bright costumes warn others that they are not fit for consumption. Blue and black make a rigorous combination that is at least touchable, if not edible, in beads. The black of DB-001 looks like hematite, not solid black. **Delicas: DB-730, DB-1497, DB-001**

216. Black Widow

It's coded into our DNA to recoil from this combination when the red is shaped like an hourglass! To make red leap from the black background, choose an opaque bead with a reflective finish, like DB-295. The black is a matte finish that absorbs light, so it recedes. Black onyx and red jasper (or red coral) provide the most saturated, powerful version of these colors. **Delicas: DB-310, DB-295**

Fancy Dangle Bracelet

Designed and created by Robin Atkins

How-to photographs by Robin Atkins

EASY

Colorful headpin elements attached to the bracelet with jump rings suggest the graceful tentacles of an anemone. If you've ever enjoyed wearing a charm bracelet, you'll love the sound and movement of these attractive dangles.

The sea anemone's otherworldly form and colors inspired Robin Atkins to design this delightful bracelet with tentacle-like dangles.

FINISHED LENGTH:
7" TO 7 1/2", DEPENDING ON CLASP

Materials
- thirty 1 1/2" long headpins, gold-filled or gold color
- fourteen 1" long headpins, gold-filled or gold color
- forty-four 4mm soldered jump rings, gold-filled or gold color
- fourty-nine strands 10" medium weight Soft Touch beading wire,
- two crimp beads, gold-filled or gold color
- selection of small beads and crystals ranging in size from 2mm to 6mm in colors to match the palette (figure 1)
- forty-five 4mm bicone crystals, alexandrite or light purple
- bracelet clasp, gold-filled or gold color

Tools
- round-nosed pliers
- wire nipper
- chain-nosed pliers
- crimping tool

217. Anemone of Another World

This anemone startles us with its brilliant complementary harmony, chartreuse and fuchsia, which could have come straight from a teen fashion magazine. The ivory tones fill out the scheme, adding richness. **Delicas: DB-203, DB-910, DB-073, DB-281**

The fun part of this project is to select beads that closely match the colors of the anemone tentacles, and which graduate in size from 2mm at the tips of the tentacles to about 6mm at the base. My initial bead selection (figure 1) included more colors than I ended up using.

Once you've selected your beads, begin arranging them on the headpins. On the longer headpins, start with fuchsia, graduate to purple, then to green beads. You can vary the arrangements slightly (figure 2), or make them all the same if you have a limited selection of beads. For an average-sized bracelet (approximately 7 1/2"), you will need thirty of the longer units.

Figure 1

Figure 2

Figure 3

Arrange cream, peach, pink, tan and lavender beads on the shorter headpins. They can vary (figure 3) or be identical. Make fourteen of these shorter units.

When all of the headpins are arranged, bend the cut end of the pin at a right angle to the last bead on each of the pins (figure 4, left pin). Using a wire nipper, nip the wire at the end of each pin leaving about $^1/4$th to $^3/8$th inch of wire from the right angle bend (figure 4, right pin). Using round-nosed pliers, grasp the very tip of the cut end of the pin wire with the tips of the pliers (figure 5). Holding the beaded headpin in your non-dominant hand and the pliers in your dominant hand, roll the pliers toward the right angle bend to form a loop (figure 6).

Figure 4

Figure 5

When all the headpins are complete with a loop at the top, insert a jump ring into each of the loops. I like to use soldered jump rings for security reasons, but you could substitute split rings or non-soldered rings. To insert the ring, grasp the open half of the loop in the chain nosed pliers, and twist (not spread) open. Insert the ring. Re-grasp the open half of the loop, and twist back to the closed position.

Arrange the headpin units with two longer ones followed by a shorter one. Repeat this sequence until all the headpin units are in a line ending with two longer ones (figure 7). If you have varied the beads on the headpins, space out the different versions evenly.

Using a crimp bead and crimping tool, attach a soldered jump ring (or one end of your clasp) to one end of a 10-inch piece of medium-weight stringing wire. Using your

Figure 6

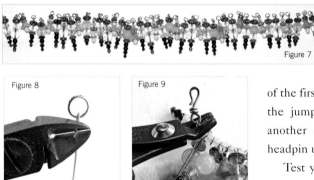

Figure 7

wire nipper, nip the tail end of the stringing wire flush with the crimp bead (figure 8).

String through one 4mm bicone crystal, then through the jump ring of the first headpin unit, then another crystal, then the jump ring of the next headpin unit, then another crystal, etc., alternating crystals with headpin units and ending with a crystal (figure 9).

Figure 8

Figure 9

Test your bracelet for length. If it is too long, remove a few headpin units and crystals, and retest. If it is too short, make and string a few more headpin units alternating with crystals, until the bracelet fits you correctly. When testing, be sure to allow for the length of the clasp.

After adjusting the bracelet to the correct length, use the crimping tool and a crimp bead to attach the clasp (figure 10).

Movement, which comes from using jump rings, and from the colors, is the charm of this piece. Use the same technique to make a lovely fringe necklace.

Figure 10

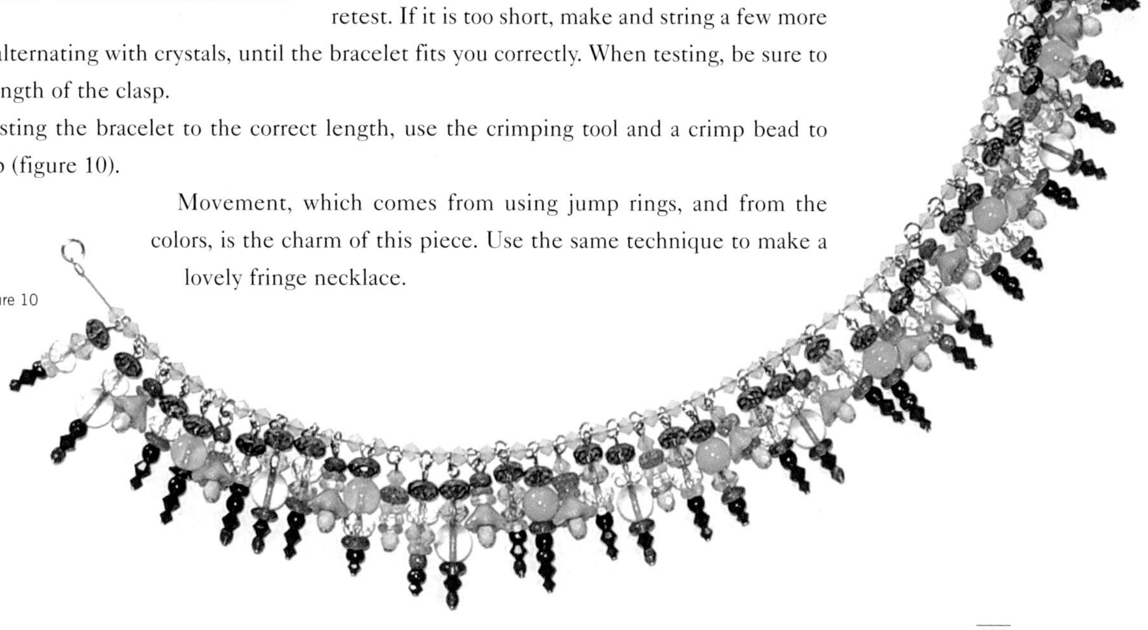

Seed Bead Swag Necklace

Designed and created by SaraBeth Cullinan

INTERMEDIATE

SaraBeth Cullinan drapes the sophisticated neutrals worn by the barn owl into elegant seed beads swags. Ivory, brown, and black combine to make a versatile and very wearable color scheme.

Elegant pearl and crystal swags drape around a ladder-stitched foundation of 8o Delica beads.

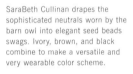

218. Owl Feathers

Ivory tones create an elegant, versatile background color. Build it up with charcoal gray, and chocolate and coppery browns. Highlight with black to make a beautiful, easy-to-work-with palette.
Delicas: DB-203, DB-749, DB-734, DB-461, DB-310

FINISHED LENGTH: 14"

Materials
• 2 to 3 gms DB-352 Matte Ivory size 8o Delica beads
• 10 gms DB-571-G/L Opal Ivory 11o seed beads
• 1/2 gram DB-571-G/L Opal Ivory 15o seed beads
• twenty-five 3mm Swarovski crystal bicones, golden shadow
• fifteen 3mm Swarovski crystal bicones, smokey topaz
• fifteen 3mm Swarovski crystal bicones, jet
• twenty-five 4mm Swarovski crystal bicones, jet
• fifteen 5mm Swarovski crystal bicones, smoky quartz
• eleven 4mm Swarovski round crystals, golden shadow
• twenty-five 3 x 5 Czech crystal rondelles, smokey topaz

• eleven 6mm fire polish rounds, brown luster
• twenty-five 8mm baroque Cultura pearls, ivory
• two sterling silver clam shell bead tips
• four sterling silver crimp tubes
• two sterling silver 8mm jump rings
• size D Nymo in matching color
• size 12 beading needle
• Seven inches .014 beading wire
• one barn owl toggle

Tools
• wire cutters
• crimping pliers

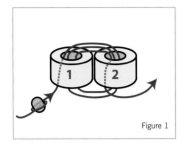

Figure 1

Using 11" of thread (or shorter if that is more comfortable) string on a stopper bead leaving a 3" to 4" tail. Start with two of the 8o Delicas (figure 1) and ladder stitch together 65 to make a 7⅝" long strip (figure increase or shorten length by increments of five.

To make the loop, string five 11o seed beads, one pearl, one bead tip and one seed bead (figure 2a). Skipping the seed bead, pass back through the bead tip and pearl. Add five seed beads and needle down into the opposite side of the same 8o Delica that loop is exiting from. Reinforce.

Edging

To begin making three-bead picot edging on the top of the ladder, loop around the connecting thread between and beneath Delicas 64 and 65. Needle up through bead 65 so you are on top of the ladder as (figure 3).

Pick up three 11o seed beads and pass the needle under the thread between 8o Delicas 64 and 65 and up through 11o seed bead #3. Next pick up two 11o seed beads and pass the needle under the thread between 8o Delicas 64 and 63 and up through the last 11o seed bead you put on the needle. Continue until you reach the opposite side of the ladder.

Repeat instructions for figure 2a to make a matching loop on the opposite side of the ladder.

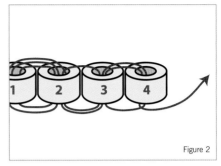

Figure 2

Figure 2a

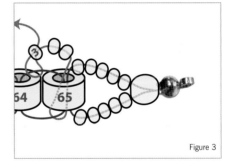

Figure 3

Fringe

Exit from the bottom of first Delica 8o and string on:

fifteen size 11o seed beads
one golden shadow 3mm bicone crystal
one smokey topaz 3mm bicone crystal
one jet 3mm bicone crystal,
one golden shadow 4mm round crystal
one jet 4mm bicone crystal
one 3x5mm smoky topaz crystal rondelle
one smoky quartz 5mm bicone crystal
one pearl
three size 15o seed beads

Note: All the fringe in this necklace is made in the same "skip-the-seed-beads-and-pass-back-through" method.

Weave back to exit from 3rd Delica 8o and string on:

one size 11o seed bead
one fire polish
one pearl
three size 15o seed beads

The last three size 15o seed beads are considered "turn beads," and you will skip them and pass back through the pearl and all the crystal beads, exiting from the golden shadow 3mm crystal. String on fifteen seed beads and needle into the fifth Delica 8o.

Close-up of end of necklace

Needle back into the same Delica 8o that this short fringe is exiting from then weave over to exit from the bottom of the sixth Delica 8o and string on:

three size 11o seed beads
one golden shadow 3mm bicone crystal
one jet 4mm bicone crystal
one pearl
three size 15o seed beads

Needle back into the same Delica 8o that the fringe is exiting from then weave over to exit from the 7th Delica 8o.

Continue making the fringe following the fringe instructions above, increasing by three beads until reaching the center (see close-up of end of necklace). Then decrease each fringe by three seed beads. For example, layer one using the 6mm fire polish starts out with one seed bead and then increase to 4, 7, 10, 13, 16, 13, 10, 7, 4

Layer 2: Shorter crystal and pearl fringe: 2, 5, 8, 11, 14, 14, 11, 8, 5, 2.

Layer 3: Longest fringe: 15, 18, 21, 24, 27, 30, 27, 24, 21, 18, 15.

Knot, clip, and bury thread.

Close the knot covers and attach to the jump rings. Using a crimp tube, attach a 3¹/₄" piece of beading wire to the jump ring and string on one each of the following:

golden shadow 3mm crystal bicone
smokey topaz 3mm crystal bicone
jet 3mm crystal bicone
golden shadow 4mm round crystal
jet 4mm crystal bicone
smokey topaz 3x5mm crystal rondelle
smokey quartz 5mm crystal bicone
pearl
smokey quartz 5mm crystal bicone
smokey topaz 3x5mm crystal rondelle
jet 4mm crystal bicone
golden shadow 4mm round crystal
jet 3mm crystal bicone
smokey topaz 3mm crystal bicone
golden shadow 3mm crystal bicone

Closure with owl toggle clasp

Sparkling Draped Loop Collar

Designed and created by Margie Deeb

INTERMEDIATE

You'll be surprised at how easy this stunning necklace is to make. This works up beautifully in solid colors as well as the patterned version shown here.

The Japanese beetle, with its carapace of glowing earthy metallics, inspired Margie Deeb to make this luxurious draped collar based on an old Miriam Haskell necklace. Want a matching ensemble? Try the Radiant Sun earrings on page 28.

218. Japanese Beetle

I added gold to the rich, robust colors of the Japanese Beetle because it takes the scheme from insect land to the world of high fashion. What unusual and striking jewelry can be made from this offbeat combination. **Delicas: DB-461, DB-125, DB-910, DB-031, DB-010**

FINISHED LENGTH: 25"

Materials
• one 16" strand 4mm faceted rounds, light green carmen
• one 16" strand 4mm faceted rounds, emerald green
• six 16" strands 6mm faceted rounds, bronze
• one 16" strand 6mm faceted round, light green carmen
• four 16" strands 8mm faceted rounds, bronze
• two 16" strands 8mm faceted rounds, light green carmen
• size D Nymo thread, brown
• size 12 sharp needle
• 2-strand clasp

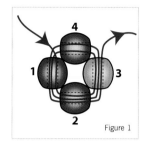

Figure 1

Foundation Choker

With a 36" piece of thread, stitch 6mm beads together with the single needle right-angle weave. Pass your needle through two bronze, one light green carmen, and one bronze bead. Secure these four beads together by circling through all of them twice. Exit through the third bead (figure 1).

Add three bronze beads and circle through them as shown in figure 2. Continue adding three beads and circling through (figure 3). From now on, we'll use the middle beads as reference points and refer to them by number with bead #1M being the first bead you strung. Continue stringing groups of three beads, alternating the color of each middle bead from bronze to light green carmen, until your foundation choker is made up of forty-three middle beads. If you have more than 4" of thread left over, leave a tail to use for adding the clasp. If not, weave what is left back into the beads, knot between beads, and cut thread.

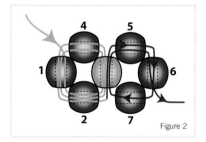

Figure 2

Figure 3

Stringing Pattern:

LG = Light Green Carmen

EG = Emerald Green Carmen

B = Bronze

Loops #1 - #4 and Loops #36 - #39: (1) 4mm LG; (1) 4mm EG; (3) 6mm B; (1) 4mm EG; (1) 4mm LG

Loop #5 and Loop #35: (1) 4mm LG; (1) 4mm EG; (4) 6mm B; (1) 4mm EG; (1) 4mm LG

Loop #6 and Loop #34: (1) 4mm LG; (1) 4mm EG; (5) 6mm B; (1) 4mm EG; (1) 4mm LG

Loop #7 and Loop #33: (1) 4mm LG; (1) 4mm EG; (6) 6mm B; (1) 4mm EG; (1) 4mm LG

Loop #8 and Loop #32: (1) 4mm LG; (1) 4mm EG; (7) 6mm B; (1) 4mm EG; (1) 4mm LG

Loop #9 and Loop #31: (1) 4mm LG; (1) 4mm EG; (8) 6mm B; (1) 4mm EG; (1) 4mm LG

Loop #10 and Loop #30: (1) 4mm LG; (1) 4mm EG; (9) 6mm B; (1) 4mm EG; (1) 4mm LG

Loop #11 and Loop #29: (1) 4mm LG; (1) 4mm EG; (3) 6mm B; (1) 6mm LG; (1) 8mm B; (1) 6mm LG; (3) 6mm B; (1) 4mm EG; (1) 4mm LG

Loop #12 and Loop #28: (1) 4mm LG; (1) 4mm EG; (3) 6mm B; (1) 6mm LG; (2) 8mm LG; (1) 6mm LG; (3) 6mm B; (1) 4mm EG; (1) 4mm LG

Loop #13 and Loop #27: (1) 4mm LG; (1) 4mm EG; (3) 6mm B; (1) 6mm LG; (1) 8mm B; (1) 8mm LG; (1) 8mm B; (1) 6mm LG; (3) 6mm B; (1) 4mm EG; (1) 4mm LG

Loop #14 and Loop #26: (1) 4mm LG; (1) 4mm EG; (3) 6mm B; (1) 6mm LG; (1) 8mm B; (2) 8mm LG; (1) 8mm B; (1) 6mm LG; (3) 6mm B; (1) 4mm EG; (1) 4mm LG

Loop #15 and Loop #25: (1) 4mm LG; (1) 4mm EG; (3) 6mm B; (1) 6mm LG; (2) 8mm B; (1) 8mm LG; (2) 8mm B; (1) 6mm LG; (3) 6mm B; (1) 4mm EG; (1) 4mm LG

Loop #16 and Loop #24: (1) 4mm LG; (1) 4mm EG; (3) 6mm B; (1) 6mm LG; (2) 8mm B; (2) 8mm LG; (2) 8mm B; (1) 6mm LG; (3) 6mm B; (1) 4mm EG; (1) 4mm LG

Loop #17 and Loop #23: (1) 4mm LG; (1) 4mm EG; (3) 6mm B; (1) 6mm LG; (3) 8mm B; (1) 8mm LG; (3) 8mm B; (1) 6mm LG; (3) 6mm B; (1) 4mm EG; (1) 4mm LG

Loop #18 and Loop #22: (1) 4mm LG; (1) 4mm EG; (3) 6mm B; (1) 6mm LG; (3) 8mm B; (2) 8mm LG; (3) 8mm B; (1) 6mm LG; (3) 6mm B; (1) 4mm EG; (1) 4mm LG

Loop #19 and Loop #21: (1) 4mm LG; (1) 4mm EG; (3) 6mm B; (1) 6mm LG; (3) 8mm B; (3) 8mm LG; (3) 8mm B; (1) 6mm LG; (3) 6mm B; (1) 4mm EG; (1) 4mm LG

Loop #20 (CENTER LOOP): (1) 4mm LG; (1) 4mm EG; (3) 6mm B; (1) 6mm LG; (3) 8mm B; (4) 8mm LG; (3) 8mm B; (1) 6mm LG; (3) 6mm B; (1) 4mm EG; (1) 4mm LG

Drape the Loops

Working from left to right, you'll drape thirty-nine loops from the bottom row of choker beads (figure 4). Note that the bottom row of choker beads are numbered 1, 2, etc., left to right. This is done for ease of counting once you get started.

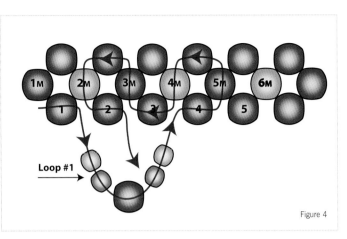

Figure 4

Weave a 36" length of thread into the beginning of the choker so that it exits the right side of bead #1 as shown in Figure 4. Add the Loop #1 beads (see stringing pattern) and pass needle into bead #4. Follow the thread path in Figure 4 until your needle exits bead #2.

Make the second loop (note in the stringing pattern that the first four loops have the same pattern), and pass needle through bead #5. Make all loops this way, exiting the right side of the bottom choker row bead that is to the right of the last loop you made.

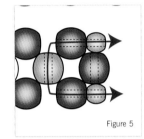

Figure 5

Add the clasp by attaching one 4mm light green carmen bead next to the last 6mm bronze on each end (figure 5 and figure 6.) Wrap the thread around the clasp and pass through the beads as many times as possible to make secure. Weave leftover thread back into the beads, knot between beads, and cut thread (figure 7).

Figure 6

Figure 7

Multi-strand Pendant & Tassel Necklace

Designed and created by Mary Hicklin

INTERMEDIATE

> A complex multi-strand necklace employs peyote stitched fringed tassels, hand-carved gemstone and lampwork beads, and silver. This project and its colors are for advanced stringing and colorists.

220. Elephant Hawk Moth

You have to be brave to work with this wild palette! The moth itself wears mustard-brown (DB-911) rather than chartreuse green, but like Mary has done in her necklace, I am adding it (DB-910) as a bridge between the pinks and the mustard. It breathes life into the palette while unifying all other colors. Use the brown accent sparingly, or eliminate it altogether.
Delicas: DB-914, DB-236, DB-911, DB-910, DB-248, DB-352, DB-287

The luxurious tones of the Elephant Hawk Moth inspired Mary Hicklin to create this unusual multi-strand necklace based on handmade beads she commissioned from Karen Ovington.

FINISHED LENGTH: APPROXIMATELY 19"

Materials

- three 20mm x 40mm handmade beads, pinks and greens of the elephant hawkmoth (right)
- one strand 6mm grossular faceted cylinders, garnet (GGFC)
- one strand 5mm grossular faceted rounds, garnet (GGFR)
- nine 10mm x 8mm grossular lozenges, garnet (GGL)
- forty-eight 6mm faceted rose quartz (RQ)
- eight 6mm faceted rhodonite (FR)
- 10mm round rhodonite (RR)
- sixteen sterling silver beads (SSB)
- eighteen medium sterling silver spacers (MSSS)
- sixteen small sterling silver spacers (SSSS)
- Sterling silver hook-and-eye closure
- 5 gms 15o Japanese seed beads in matching greens and pinks
- 1 gram 8/o beads to fill large holes in handmade beads, if needed
- 2 gms tiny tourmalines for fringe (flat disks, cubes, etc.)
- two sterling silver necklace cones
- 4" 16g sterling round wire, optional for handmade hook closure:
- 8" 18g sterling round wire, optional for wired cones:

- 20" 20g sterling round wire, optional for wire work extension
- optional extension–rather than making an extension from wire, use a commercial sterling chain with holes large enough for hook closure
- .024/49 strand (heavy) Soft Touch beading wire
- eight crimps sized for the beading cable
- silk to match two shorter strands of beads
- size D Nymo beading thread
- size 13beading needles
- wire needles for silk
- G-S Hypo Cement or your preferred fusing method
- beeswax to condition beading thread

Tools

- safety glasses (always wear when cutting wire or cable, especially when trimming small bits)
- cable cutters
- wire cutters, optional
- Chain-nose pliers, optional
- Round-nose pliers, optional
- jeweler's hammer, optional
- small anvil, optional
- small file, optional

The longest strand, which holds the handmade beads and tassel, is strung on cable for strength. Cut a length of bead cable sized for the beads with the smallest holes and twice the length you will need. (Because cable frays when passed through hand-drilled stone beads you will need to trim the end as you progress.)

To make the tassel, select a handmade bead and handmade disk. Using a piece of scrap beading cable 6" long, make a small loop to hold the fringe, finish with a crimp. (See page 170 for crimping instructions). The loop and crimp should fit inside the handmade bead.

Attach as many fringes as you like to the loop, in as many styles as you wish. The pattern for one of the fringes I used is on page 144.

String a large handmade bead onto the cable, pull the loop with the fringe up inside the bead to cover the fringe attachments. The large bead should rest securely upon the top of the fringe with the knots and loop hidden inside the bead and with enough fringe to secure it permanently. If the holes of the handmade beads are large, string 8/o beads on the cable to fill the hole in the handmade bead (figure 1).

String 1 GGFC, 1 handmade disk bead, 1 GGFC

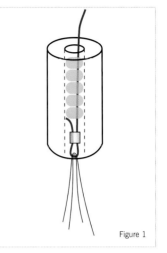

Figure 1

Top of Tassel

Option #1 (figure 2): You may simply make a loop and string the necklace cable through it. To finish the top of the tassel in this way:

- String 1 decorative crimp bead
- String enough seed beads onto the cable for a small loop
- Pass the cable back through the crimp and some of the tassel beads if possible
- Tighten the cable, crimp the crimp bead
- Cut off excess cable
- Attach the finished tassel to the cable you set aside

Option #2 (shown in finished photo): Cover the loop with a beaded embellished bead, as I have done, which will serve as a central element on the longest necklace strand. First finish the tassel as follows:

- String 1 crimp bead
- Pass the cable back through it (and some of the beads if possible) leaving a small loop for attachment to the necklace strand
- Tighten carefully, without letting the loop close, crimp the crimp bead
- Cut off excess cable

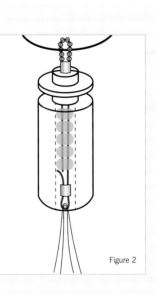

Figure 2

You must make the beaded bead before you continue to assemble the necklace as the necklace cable must pass through the middle of it. See directions for making the free-hand gourd stitched beaded bead on page 144.

Longest Strand

Because the tassel is already attached to the cable, work from the center to the ends. If you crimped the two ends together, cut the crimp off. Be careful that the tassel does not come off as you string the beads. If the two handmade beads are not the same length, adjust the number of GGFC beads on one side so both sides are equal in length.

Stringing Pattern (1/2):

one SSB
nine GGFC
one SSB
one RR
one SSB
nine GGFC
one SSB
one handmade bead
one SSB
nine GGFC
one SSB
one RR
one SSB
nine GGFC
one SSB
one RR

Attach a temporary crimp on the end of the cable to secure the beads. Repeat stringing pattern for the other side.

Make sure both sides are symmetrical and adjust as necessary. Close with temporary crimps at the cable tips, which you will cut off before finishing. Use one crimp on each rather than crimping the ends together to facilitate measuring against the other strands.

Middle strand

Cut an appropriate size/color silk three to four times the length of finished strand, place temporary knot at end. Use a single or double strand as appropriate for your beads. String eight pink seed beads, which will be hidden under finishing cone.

Stringing Pattern:

one MSSS
one GGL
one MSS
six RQ

Repeat seven times

one MSSS
one GGL
one MSSS
eight pink seed beads

Move the beads to the center of the silk. Because handcut stone beads vary in size, you'll need to adjust the arrangement and length. Make adjustments as necessary.

Start knotting at the center and work outward to each end. Make a pearl knot between each bead. Check each knot carefully to ensure it is tight and there are no unsightly gaps before moving to the next bead. As you get near the ends, keep checking the length and position of the central bead carefully—it is very difficult to remove a tightened pearl knot. Correct the number of beads as necessary.

Shortest Strand

On appropriate size/color silk string eight green seed beads, which will be hidden under cone.

Move the beads to the center of the silk. Check the arrangement and length, string more or remove beads as necessary. Knot as described for middle strand.

Stringing Pattern:

four GGFR
b: one SSSS
c: one FR
d: one SSSS
e: six GGFR

Repeat pattern b through e 6 times

one SSSS
one FR
one SSSS
four GGFR
eight green seed beads

Finish strand ends with sterling necklace cones on wire.

Attach cones as shown on page 171.

Finish hook and eye sides (figure 3.)

Figure 3

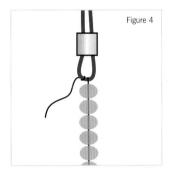

Figure 4

2-bead flower stems

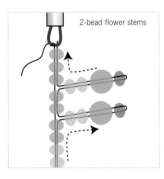

3-bead flower stems

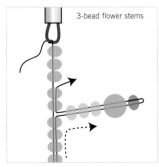

Branched Tourmaline Flower Fringe Pattern

This fringe element has "stems" with tiny tourmaline flowers. The stems gradually lengthen then branch toward the top.

Cut a convenient length of Nymo D. If using Japanese 15o you should be able to double the thread for strength.

Wax thread, tie the end to the cable loop. Glue the knot with G-S Cement, leave the tail to weave in later. String 4 1/2" of dark brownish green 15o seed beads for the length of the fringe (figure 4). You'll create stems and branches from this length.

2-bead stems: String two dark brownish green seed beads for flower stem, one tourmaline, one pink seed bead. Go back through tourmaline and two seed beads of the flower stem, then through 2 seed beads of the main stem, working upwards, leaving the needle in position to start the next stem. As you pull the thread up through the central stem pull it up tightly each time. This will help the fringe to curl. Repeat nine times (figure 5).

3-bead stems: String three seed beads for flower stem, one tourmaline, one pink seed bead, go back through tourmaline and three seed beads of the stem then through two beads of the main stem, working upward. Repeat nine times.

4-bead stems (page 144): String four stem seed beads, one tourmaline, one pink seed bead, go back through tourmaline and four seed beads of the stem then through two beads of the main stem, working upward. Repeat nine times.

Figure 5

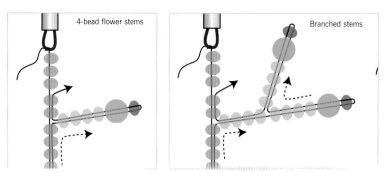

Branched stems: Main branch: String eight flower stem seed beads, one tourmaline, one pink seed bead, go back through tourmaline and four seed beads. Mini-branch: String four stem seed beads, one tourmaline, one pink seed bead, go back through tourmaline, four seed beads of this mini-branch, four seed beads of main branch, four seed beads of central stem. Repeat to top of fringe.

Make additional fringes. Weave tails into central stems, fuse, and trim.

Figure 6

Freehand Peyote Beaded Bead for Tassel Attachment

It looks nice to cover the tassel attachment loop with a round bead-like element (figure 6). The necklace cable will go through its center as though it had a hole. This beaded bead is hollow and will not be as perfectly round as one worked over a form, but it doesn't matter because it will be embellished with a nice ruffle. 15o Japanese round beads work best.

Tubular single drop peyote stitch is used to make the bead, with increases to make the bead shape. As you work each round, keep good tension on the thread so the resulting bead will hold its shape. Keep shaping the bead as you go. You will build up the bead shape from below the crimp on the tassel loop by increasing. When the edges of the bead are even with the loop, you will string the necklace cable through the loop and cover it with more rows of peyote stitch. Then you will decrease to dome and close the top of the bead.

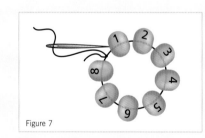

Figure 7

Rounds 1 and 2:

With doubled Nymo D, string eight green seed beads and tie into a round below the loop crimp. Leave tails to weave in later (figure 7). Step up to next row by going back through 1st bead strung.

Round 3:

1. Increase in the first space (string two beads instead of one), go through the third bead strung as usual.
2. Single bead in next space
3. Increase in next space
4. Single bead in last space
5. Step up to the next row by going through first bead of first increase.

Round 4:

1. Single bead between the two beads of the first increase
2. Increase in next space
3. Increase in next space
4. Single bead between the two beads of the second increase
5. Increase
6. Increase
7. Step up to the next row

Round 5 – work even, no increases:
1. Single bead
2. Single bead between two beads of previous increase
3. Repeat around
4. Step up to the next row

Round 6 – increase every other space:
1. Increase
2. Single bead
3. Repeat around
4. Step up to the next row

Round 7 – work even, no increases:
1. One bead between the two beads of the increase
2. Single
3. Single
4. Continue around
5. Step up to the next row
6. Attach tassel to the necklace cable.

Assuming the edges of the beaded bead are up to the tassel loop (if not, work another row or two), attach the tassel to the beading cable prepared for the longest strand. Crimp the ends of the cable together near the tips using a waste crimp. This will prevent the tassel from slipping off the cable. Once the beaded bead is complete, it is very difficult to pass the cable through the bead and the tassel loop inside, so don't let it fall off!

Lay the cable across the beaded bead and bead Round 8 over it.

Round 8:
**(fifteen spaces to fill,
cable should sit in spaces 1 and 7)**
1. Single bead in each space around,
   over the cable in spaces 1 and 7
2. Step up to the next row

Round 9 – work even:
1. Single bead in each space around
2. Step up to the next row

Round 10:
1. Decrease (run thread through the
   two beads as usual, without a bead on it)
2. Single bead
3. Single bead
4. Repeat previous three steps around
5. Step up by going through both beads
   of the first decrease

Round 11:
1. Single bead
2. Single bead across decrease
3. Continue around
4. Step up

Round 12:
1. Decrease
2. Single bead
3. Single bead
4. Repeat previous three steps around
5. Step up

Round 13:
1. Single around
2. Step up

Round 14:
1. Close off top

Ruffle Decoration

To start a wavy ruffle around the beaded bead, first visualize it. Then start anywhere on the beaded bead, run the needle through a bead, string one dark green seed bead, go through one of the adjacent beads as though doing normal gourd stitch. String another dark green bead but do not follow the line of the underlying gourd stitch, instead connect to an adjacent bead on an attractive angle. Continue as the spirit moves you, it is not necessary to wind up at the starting point. When you have a nice wavy line, turn back and work gourd stitch over the newly added beads, increasing every other bead. At the end of each pass, add another bead onto the beaded bead so the ruffle tapers at the ends.

Repeat two to four times to make a ruffle around the bead, shading successive rows from dark green to light green to pink. Keep tight tension so the decoration ruffles up.

And/or embellish the beaded bead with other beads, small pearls, etc.

Weave ends in, glue or fuse knots.

INSPIRATION

&

TECHNIQUES

Extraordinary use of color emerges from both knowledge and a depth of personal expression. No matter how often the muse gifts you, you must have the ability to rise to her bequest. You need ability to express inspiration. Many artists study color their entire lives. Their knowledge expands their mastery so that intuition and expression may come into play.

Finding your voice, through color or any other medium, is a lifelong process. There are no guaranteed paths, as the process is a personal journey, and ultimately, a spiritual one. It requires that you allow all your senses to find the beauty, movement, light, and life of color, wherever it exists. It requires passion.

Use the basic techniques in this section to launch and expand your mastery, and let the artwork inspire your artistry.

Turquoise, amethyst, silver; hand
charm by Mythmakers
Necklace by Margie Deeb

Necklace by Jamie Cloud Eakin
Yellow agate, dendritic opal, citrine

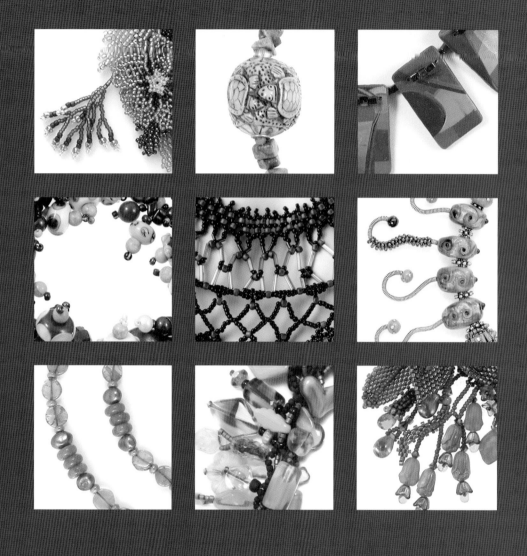

INSPIRATION GALLERY

Photograph by Cheryl Cobern-Browne

In a pocket of the Irish coastline where the Gulf Stream mingles with the Atlantic, a copper statue stands draped in dapples of pink, red, and orange on an aqua blue-green net. Cheryl-Cobern Browne has knitted the music of sea and sky and flowered landscape into *Mrs. Monn's Mantle*, a tapestry of wire, glass beads, and brass charms. Blue-greens and copper pair beautifully, and when the scarf is placed on Mrs. Monn, both come to life.

Mantle photograph by Haigwood Studios

No less spectacular in color than this dragonfly perched on a bud's snout is Margo Field's *Poppies* from her Garden Varieties series. A multitude of yellow-greens, from dark to light and muted to bright, intensify orange and coral tones. Specks of mauve-purple accent the fringe like a dusting of pollen. Margo combines color, texture, and detail into a rich, harmonious bouquet. Glass seed beads

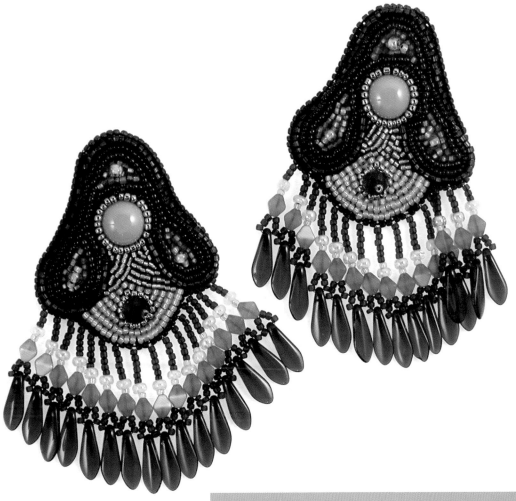

Super-rich tones forge a sumptuous palette for these unusual bell-shaped earrings. Margie Deeb brings tones steeped in the cooler, darker side of the color wheel to life by juxtaposing them against sparks of warm, bright gold. Lavender is the only member of this palette not intensely saturated. Amethyst, turquoise, 24kt gold, and glass beads

Festive Time Robin Atkins augments the graphic boldness of this architectural photo palette by including light green. In choosing mostly opaque glass she creates a dense, textural mass of colorful high jinks. Vintage and new pressed glass, lampworked beads

iStockphoto.com / AVTG

Jeannette Cook breathes life into her *May's Garden Necklace* with unexpected shades of bright blue. Though not the dominant force, it is the color that rhythmically dances your gaze across the entire piece with its bursts of brilliance. Cook rounds out the palette by including sparks of bright yellow and fuchsia.

Vintage pressed glass, seed beads, red coral; right angle weave, peyote, and indebele stitch

A Lilac-Breasted Roller, one of the most beautiful birds in existence, inspired Margie Deeb's panoply of hues on a cobalt background. The color challenge this bird presented was one of abundance: so many colors, and all so gorgeous. With a calligraphic flourish of lilac, Margie swirls your attention from the main stone up toward the center, the heart of the wearer, crowned in turquoise. The unique shape suggests arms raised in praise of color and beauty.
Chrysocolla, turquoise, amethyst, chalcedony, vintage pressed glass, 24kt and glass beads

Carol Cypher uses four highly contrasting colors to make one stunning piece. The contrasts rivet your attention, just as it does in the Alaskan totem carving.
Lampwork by Carol Cypher
Glass beads and sterling clasp

In *Warm*, by Lisa Niven Kelly, color, shape and design unite with glass and metal to spawn a living organism. It is in the details that this creature comes to life. Subtle neutral tones of weathered wood and rust inhabit amoebic shaped beads. Copper stardust highlights primordial whorls specked with eye-like black dots. Heads sprout at the end of coiled tendrils. At any moment the necklace will twist and wriggle its way right off the page.

Lampwork, wire work, coiling, ladder stitch, and freeform seed bead work; Moretti and dichroic glass, silver, Swarovski crystal, and seed beads

Colorful abstractions of complementary harmonies, highlighted by yellow and blue-violet, mingle into luminosity. Each tabular block of Carol Zilliacus's necklace declares itself in geometric color fields layered with translucent ghosts of iridescence. Dulled black urges orange and red to greater vibrancy, and the alchemy is one of glowing radiance.

Glass and hand made polymer clay beads designed and constructed by Carol Zilliacus.

A mother-of-pearl heart, whose surface glimmers rainbows, sets the foundation for Jamie Cloud Eakins's palette of tonally matched blues. These cool muted colors intone peace and elegance as quiet as a snow covered landscape at twilight.

Mother-of-pearl heart inlaid with abalone cabochon, freshwater pearls, blue aventurine, iolite, sterling

Kristy Nijenkamp echoes the
divine beauty of an opening
lotus blossom in her *Purple
Goddess* lampwork and gemstone necklace. The focal bead,
which encompasses all the colors of the photo and more, even
incorporates the dark dots of
the tiny crawling bugs.
Lampwork by Kristy Nijenkamp;
amethyst, fluorite, green agate

©iStockphoto.com / Miluschka Kok

©iStockphoto.com / pixonaut

Frieda's Turtle Necklace A simple, direct color inspiration can be captivating. Elizabeth Ann Scarborough takes a turtle's palette right off its shell and embellishes it with gold. The charm of this piece is in the details. Made as a gift, the necklace features five pressed glass turtles and one peyote stitched beaded turtle. Note the tiny black eyes and the pressed glass leaf for a tail.
Glass, pearls, carved bone, rhyolite

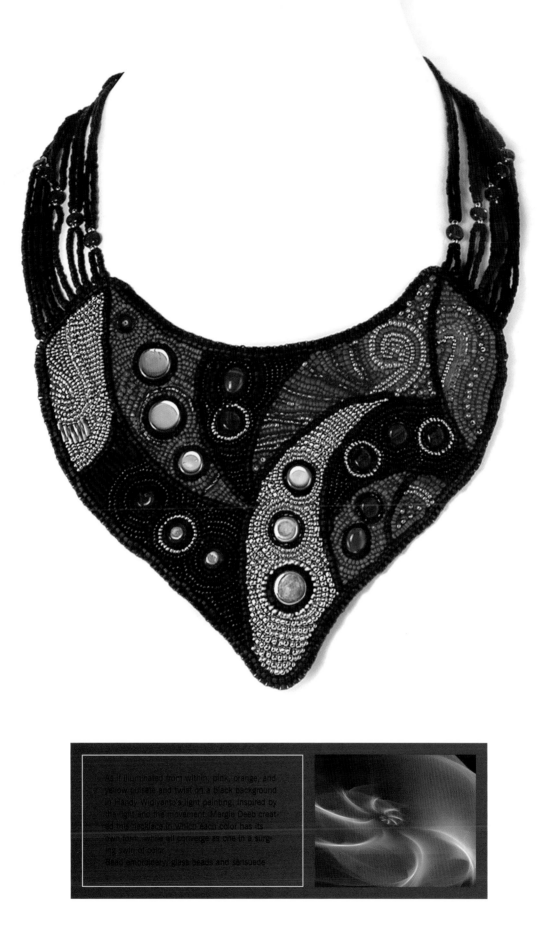

As if illuminated from within, pink, orange, and yellow pulsate and twist on a black background in Handy Widiyanto's light painting. Inspired by the light and the movement, Margie Deeb created this necklace in which each color has its own form, while all converge as one in a surging swirl of color.
Bead embroidery; glass beads and sensuede

Sun Set Colors Captured
SaraBeth Cullinan

A luxurious harmony of red, purple,
and violet embellish a stone. As in the
palette of the stained glass window,
touches of amber, in the form of citrine,
augment the palette with warmth.
Carnelian, amethyst, citrine, seed
beads used in peyote stitch
Stone photograph by Robert Still

Robin Atkins weaves
400 German pressed
glass beads from the
1940s to the1960s—no
two alike—into a feast of
color. Every aspect of
color is represented: light
and dark, vibrant and
muted, saturated and
neutral, warm and cool,
opaque and transparent,
quiet and loud. Atkins
weaves beauty and har-
mony from such diversity
with masterful attention
to design and shape, using
black as a unifying color.
Necklace photograph by
Haigwood Studios

This delicate netted neckpiece by Jean Campbell features contemporary colorings on turn-of-the-century style. Such a mass of black is prey to becoming heavy and oppressive. In this instance is does not because of the way it is used: as a graceful, scalloped web of lace and fringe. Copper-orange accents at the end of the fringe draw the eye downward and brighten the palette. Aqua-green and minute amounts of violet accentuate the curves of the piece and its wearer. Thus the title *VaVoom*.

Pressed glass, bugle and seed beads; circular netting
Necklace photograph by Haigwood Studios

Egyptian in style but decisively un-Egyptian in palette, Elizabeth Ann Scarborough's *Royal Broadcollar* wears the colors of a carnival carousel. A vibrant purple/gold scheme with bright turquoise accents surrounds the scarab-inspired dichroic cab. A smattering of iridescent finishes injects flashes of magenta, lime green, and cobalt blue. These are full-blown charged colors, currents of spectral electricity Scarborough has harnessed and transformed into a work of art.

Ladder stitched glass seed and bugle beads
Dichroic cab by Bruce St. John Maher

Mastery and finesse are required to create a cohesive look with so many different shapes and sizes. Sherry Serafini achieves unity by limiting her palette and choosing colors and surface finishes carefully. Brown, beige, and grey dominate. By using metallics and bead finishes that emit iridescent flashes of color, she subtly creates a more extended palette. Degas' ballerina is the color inspiration for *Dancing in the Shadow*. By restricting the hues to neutrals, her blue waistband becomes a stronger focal point.

Resin coated magnet, seed beads, hematite, pearls, glass

Fall Splendor
Rev. Wendy Ellsworth nestles a
snake among autumn's array of
earth colors. Red-orange, like a
vibrant jewel, is fall's most electric
hue. Here it lights up the whole
piece. With off-loom beading
Ellsworth has achieved life-like
texture in the leaves, acorns,
and snakeskin.
Herringbone stitched glass
seed beads

TECHNIQUES

BEADING BASICS

THE BASICS OF STRINGING, FINISHING, AND ON- AND OFF-LOOM WEAVING

STRINGING

Here are the basic stringing techniques you'll need to know to get started on all the projects in this book.

Stringing with Cord

Stringing beads on cord makes luxurious, supple strands that are strong. Beading cord is made of either nylon or silk (best for pearls) and consists of several strands of finer cord twisted together.

Use flexible twisted wire needles with beading cord. Twisted needles have large eyes that collapse as you pull cord through beads. They are available in several gauges, from light (for 2mm to 3mm beads) to heavy (for 8mm and larger beads).

You can also create a self-needle on thicker cord by coating an inch of the end with instant glue.

You may double the cord or keep it as a single cord. If doubling, begin with a piece about five times the length of the final necklace. If you are stringing with a single cord, use a length 2 1/2 times longer. String the cord on the needle and pull it half way through, so the needle is in the very center of the length of cord.

To attach clasps and finish strands, beading cord is knotted two or more times. The knots must be glued because cord is slippery and the knots may eventually untie. Unsightly knots must be hidden by using one of two kinds of knot covers: double-cup (clamshell) bead tips or single-cup bead tips. The technique for both is similar. Bead tips work great for light necklaces. Heavier necklaces are strongest when finished with cones (page 171).

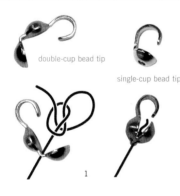

double-cup bead tip

single-cup bead tip

1

1. To securely finish each end of the strand you'll need to cover your knots with a bead tip.

Slide the bead tip onto the cord and tie a knot. Slide the knot in the base of the cup. Tie a second knot and clip the end. Tie as many knots as needed, one on top of the other, to make a bundle of knots too large to be pulled through the bead tip.

Apply jeweler's cement to the knot to keep it secure.

2

2. When the cement is dry, trim the end of the cord close to the knot, and close the cups together with chain-nose pliers.

3

3. Attach the hook of the bead tip around a clasp or jump ring. Use round-nose or chain-nose pliers to curl the hook so that its end touches the cup or basket of the bead tip.

flexible twisted wire needles

beaded cord strand finished with clamshell bead tips

chain-nose pliers

round-nose pliers

Stringing beads on wire ensures that beads with sharp-edged holes will not cut the strands. Beading wire has become so flexible that beautifully draping strands are possible.

Flexible beading wire is composed of several braided or twisted cables covered with smooth material, like plastic or nylon. It is very strong and is available in many weights. SoftFlex, Acculon, and Beadalon are reliable brands offering a range of colors.

Needles with large eyes can be used with the thinnest wire (.010 gauge), but needles are not necessary with most beading wire.

Because beading wire is often too thick to be knotted, crimp beads are used to attach clasps and finish your jewelry. Crimp beads have large holes and are made of thin metal designed to be flattened over the beading wire to secure it.

For a professional look, crimp beads must closely match the wire size used for the strand, and be made of sterling or gold (not base metal which will eventually discolor).

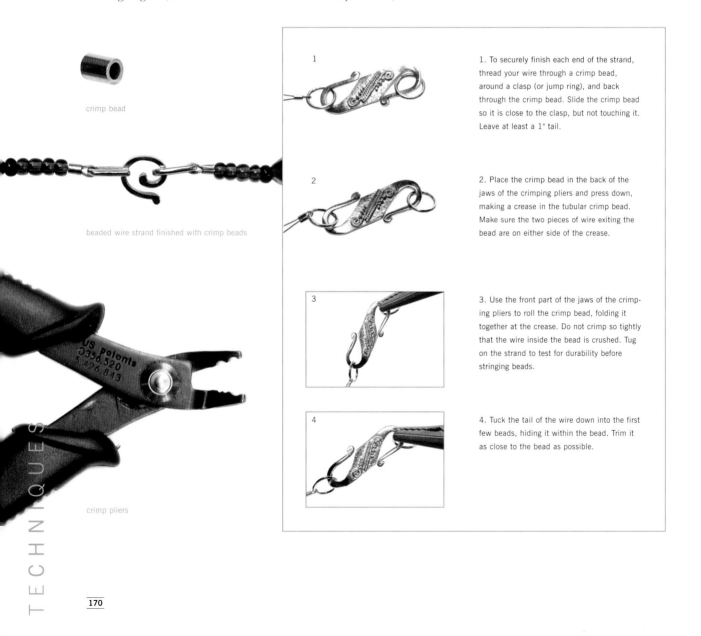

crimp bead

beaded wire strand finished with crimp beads

crimp pliers

1

2

3

4

1. To securely finish each end of the strand, thread your wire through a crimp bead, around a clasp (or jump ring), and back through the crimp bead. Slide the crimp bead so it is close to the clasp, but not touching it. Leave at least a 1" tail.

2. Place the crimp bead in the back of the jaws of the crimping pliers and press down, making a crease in the tubular crimp bead. Make sure the two pieces of wire exiting the bead are on either side of the crease.

3. Use the front part of the jaws of the crimping pliers to roll the crimp bead, folding it together at the crease. Do not crimp so tightly that the wire inside the bead is crushed. Tug on the strand to test for durability before stringing beads.

4. Tuck the tail of the wire down into the first few beads, hiding it within the bead. Trim it as close to the bead as possible.

Cones are used to hide knots and make attractive clasp connections. Finish multi-strands and strands of large, chunky beads with cones. They add an elegant taper to the ends of the strands.

various types of cones

1. You'll need to make a looped structure upon which to secure the strands. (The cone will slide over this structure.) Cut a 4" piece of 0.018- or 0.020-gauge round wire. Grasp it about 1" from the top with a pair of chain-nose pliers. Bend the top down at a right angle.

2. Just above the bend, grasp the wire with round-nose pliers. Wrap the wire in the direction opposite the bend, making a loop. Round-nose pliers enable you to form a round loop 3.

3. Pull the end of the wire toward the direction as the first bend.

4. If you wish to use jump rings, split rings, or chains, they can be added while the loop is still open. In this example, three soldered jump rings have been added. Strands will later be attached to each jump ring.

5. Close the loop by wrapping the wire around itself (underneath the loop). Clamp flat across the loop with the round-nose pliers, while using the chain-nose pliers to wrap. Make sure your first wrap is as close to the loop as possible, and each subsequent wrap butts right up against the previous one. Two are sufficient. Clip the excess wire as close to the wraps as possible.

    Note: Before attaching strands, test the size of the loop and wraps for fit. Slide the cone onto the wire, covering the loop and rings to make sure it fits properly. You may have to adjust the size of the loop or the number of wraps to make it fit within the cone properly.

clip excess

6. If you are stringing with thread or cord (as required in the *Rainforest Cascade Necklace* project (page 122), for example), this is the time to tie the bundle of thread or cord tails to the wire loop.

    Before you attach the bundle to the loop, tie all the cord tails together with two overhand knots.

    Separate the tails in half so you have two bunches of cord. Take one bunch of cords and thread it through the loop from right to left. Take the other bunch and thread it through the loop from left to right.

    Tie them together using two square knots. Seal the knots with jeweler's cement. Trim the cord ends $^1/_4$" from the knot when the cement is dry.

7. If you are attaching your strands to jump rings, do so at this time.

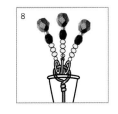

8. Slide the cone over the wire loop to conceal everything but the strands.

9. Attach the finding to the wire by making another loop, repeating steps 1 through 5. Make the right-angle bend in the wire a distance of three wraps away from the top of the cone.

10. Be sure to snug the wraps tightly against both the wire and the top of the cone, so no parts slide around. Do the same thing for the other end of the strand.

multi-strands finished with cones

Peyote and brick stitch are the most popular of all off-loom stitches. They both position the beads in brick formation, that is, staggered rather than aligned straight (like loomweaving).

Weaving is best done with multifilament nylon thread. It is available in either twisted or untwisted and comes in sizes 00 (the finest) to 0, A, B, D, and F, the heaviest. Choose a size that will pass through the beads several times. Waxing the thread with beeswax or a thread conditioner is optional, and makes thread stronger and easier to work with.

Beading needles are available in several sizes, with 10 being the largest, and 16 the smallest.

Peyote Stitch (Even-Count)

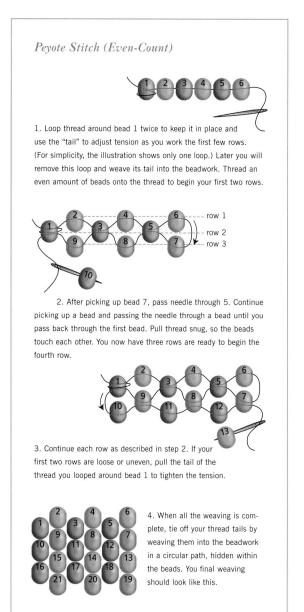

1. Loop thread around bead 1 twice to keep it in place and use the "tail" to adjust tension as you work the first few rows. (For simplicity, the illustration shows only one loop.) Later you will remove this loop and weave its tail into the beadwork. Thread an even amount of beads onto the thread to begin your first two rows.

2. After picking up bead 7, pass needle through 5. Continue picking up a bead and passing the needle through a bead until you pass back through the first bead. Pull thread snug, so the beads touch each other. You now have three rows are ready to begin the fourth row.

3. Continue each row as described in step 2. If your first two rows are loose or uneven, pull the tail of the thread you looped around bead 1 to tighten the tension.

4. When all the weaving is complete, tie off your thread tails by weaving them into the beadwork in a circular path, hidden within the beads. You final weaving should look like this.

Peyote Stitch (Odd-Count)

1. Begin with the loop as shown in step 1 of the even-count peyote. (For simplicity, the loop around the first bead is not shown in this diagram.) Place an odd number of beads onto the thread to begin your first two rows. Thread all but the last bead of row 3 into place. Pass thread through beads 1 and 2. Put bead 11 on the thread.

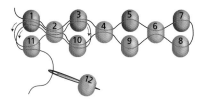

2. After you've passed back through beads 1 and 2 and picked up bead 11, you are going to make a figure-eight path with the thread to begin the fourth row. Pass thread through beads 2, 3, 10, 2, and 1, and then back through 11. If your needle's final exit bead is 11, and the beads on the left end are fit snugly together, you'll know your figure-eight path was successful. You won't have to do this fancy move again until you start a new project using the odd-count peyote.

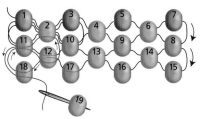

3. From here on out, each row that begins on the left has a more complex turn than the row beginning on the right. After picking up bead 18, pass the thread through beads 11, 12, 2, and 11, and back through 18 to begin the next row.

TECHNIQUES

Increasing Odd Numbered Rows of Peyote Stitch by One Bead

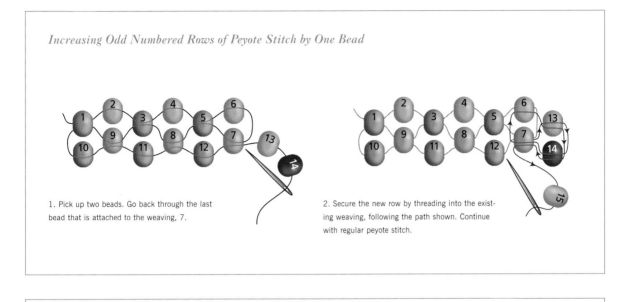

1. Pick up two beads. Go back through the last bead that is attached to the weaving, 7.

2. Secure the new row by threading into the existing weaving, following the path shown. Continue with regular peyote stitch.

Increasing Peyote Stitch by an Odd Number of Beads

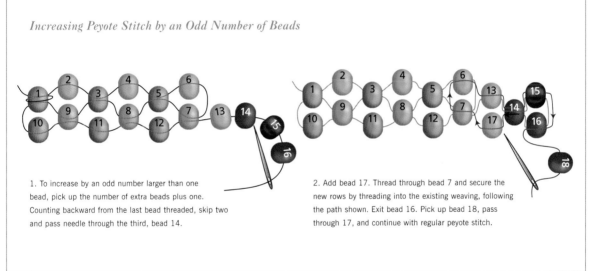

1. To increase by an odd number larger than one bead, pick up the number of extra beads plus one. Counting backward from the last bead threaded, skip two and pass needle through the third, bead 14.

2. Add bead 17. Thread through bead 7 and secure the new rows by threading into the existing weaving, following the path shown. Exit bead 16. Pick up bead 18, pass through 17, and continue with regular peyote stitch.

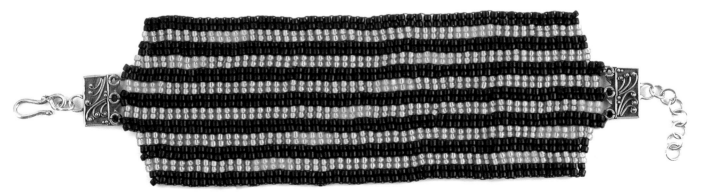

2-drop peyote in which two beads are used as one.
Bracelet by Margie Deeb

Increasing Peyote Stitch by an Even Number of Beads

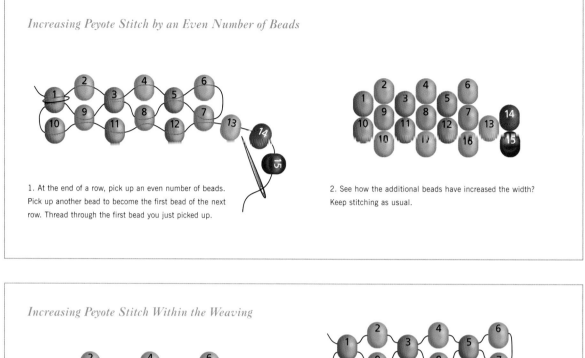

1. At the end of a row, pick up an even number of beads. Pick up another bead to become the first bead of the next row. Thread through the first bead you just picked up.

2. See how the additional beads have increased the width? Keep stitching as usual.

Increasing Peyote Stitch Within the Weaving

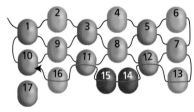

1. After exiting a bead within the piece, pick up two beads (14 and 15) and continue with regular peyote stitch.

2. When you stitch the next row, place one bead (bead 19) between the two increase beads. Continue stitching as regular. The increase beads will push the other others beads diagonally, and the width will increased two vertical rows.

Alpine Forget-Me-Nots
by Margo Field
Flowers in odd-count flat peyote, increasing in the middle and decreasing on the sides.

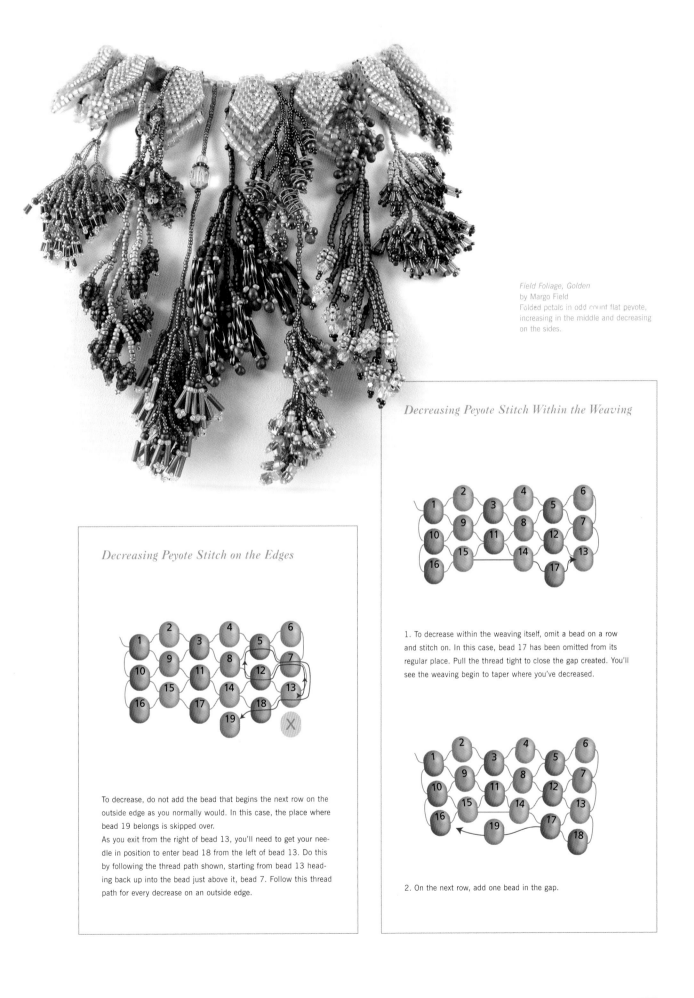

Field Foliage, Golden
by Margo Field
Folded petals in odd count flat peyote,
increasing in the middle and decreasing
on the sides.

Decreasing Peyote Stitch Within the Weaving

1. To decrease within the weaving itself, omit a bead on a row and stitch on. In this case, bead 17 has been omitted from its regular place. Pull the thread tight to close the gap created. You'll see the weaving begin to taper where you've decreased.

2. On the next row, add one bead in the gap.

Decreasing Peyote Stitch on the Edges

To decrease, do not add the bead that begins the next row on the outside edge as you normally would. In this case, the place where bead 19 belongs is skipped over.

As you exit from the right of bead 13, you'll need to get your needle in position to enter bead 18 from the left of bead 13. Do this by following the thread path shown, starting from bead 13 heading back up into the bead just above it, bead 7. Follow this thread path for every decrease on an outside edge.

1. Notice how the beads in the brick stitch are rotated 90 degrees from their position in the peyote stitch.
Begin with the loop as described in step 1 of the even-count peyote.

Your first row will be a ladder of beads stitched side by side. The thread between the beads are the rungs to which you will stitch more beads.

From the top of bead 1, go down into bead 2, back up through 1, and back down into 2. For added security, circle up through 1 and down into 2 again before adding bead 3. (For simplicity, this is not shown in the illustration.)

2. Following the thread path in the diagram, continue circling through the beads and stitching them together.

After the needle passes through each bead, it goes backward through the previous bead, and then forward again. You are making a series of loops with your thread. Every other loop starts at the top, and every other loop starts at the bottom.

This diagram shows the pattern of movement you make with your thread. Make your first row as long as desired. (In these instructions the first row–the ladder–is five beads wide.)

3. Add two beads to the thread to begin your second row. In this diagram, beads 6 and 7 have been added, and the needle will be passed under the top rung between beads 4 and 5.

Beads 6 and 7 are the beginning of the second row.

4. Position beads 6 and 7 side by side atop the ladder. Pass needle under the rung that is on top and between the last two beads of the first row, beads 4 and 5. Immediately pass the needle back up through bead 7.

The outer bead of this row, bead 6, will not be hooked onto any ladder rungs.

5. Continue attaching beads to the ladder, looping your thread under the rungs. Begin a new row the same way you did in step 4.

Notice that the outer bead of the second row, bead 11, is not hooked onto a rung, just like bead 6. The outer bead of every row will not be hooked onto a rung.

You may find it easier to flip your piece of beadwork over vertically each time you being a new row. If you do this, you'll be stitching each row in the same direction.

6. When all the weaving is complete, tie off your thread tails by weaving them into the beadwork in a circular path, hidden within the beads.

You final weaving should look like this. See how it resembles the peyote stitch rotated 90 degrees?

Notice how every other row sticks half a bead width out to the left or the right, like rows of stacked bricks.

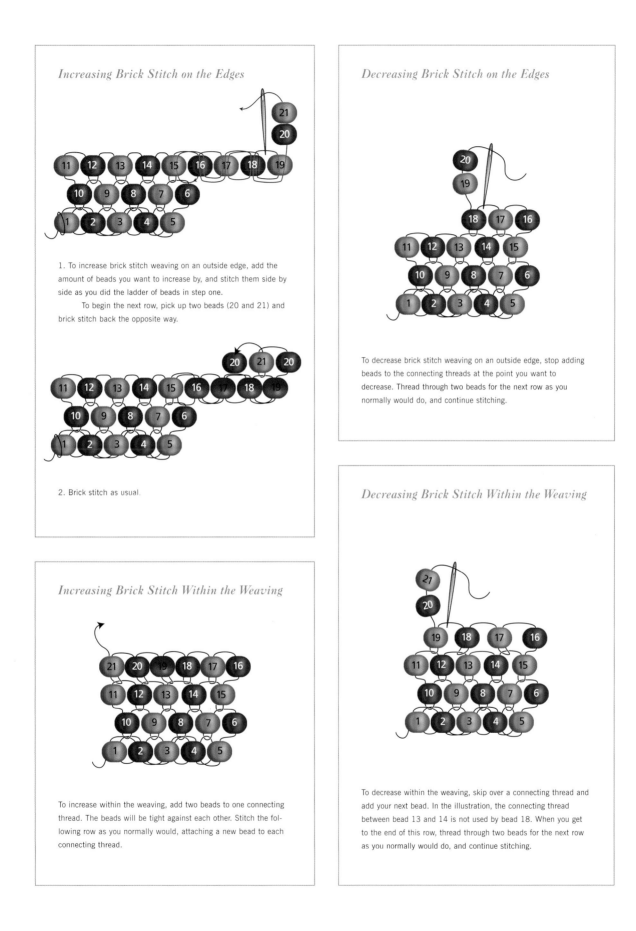

Increasing Brick Stitch on the Edges

1. To increase brick stitch weaving on an outside edge, add the amount of beads you want to increase by, and stitch them side by side as you did the ladder of beads in step one.

To begin the next row, pick up two beads (20 and 21) and brick stitch back the opposite way.

2. Brick stitch as usual.

Decreasing Brick Stitch on the Edges

To decrease brick stitch weaving on an outside edge, stop adding beads to the connecting threads at the point you want to decrease. Thread through two beads for the next row as you normally would do, and continue stitching.

Increasing Brick Stitch Within the Weaving

To increase within the weaving, add two beads to one connecting thread. The beads will be tight against each other. Stitch the following row as you normally would, attaching a new bead to each connecting thread.

Decreasing Brick Stitch Within the Weaving

To decrease within the weaving, skip over a connecting thread and add your next bead. In the illustration, the connecting thread between bead 13 and 14 is not used by bead 18. When you get to the end of this row, thread through two beads for the next row as you normally would do, and continue stitching.

LOOM WEAVING

Loom weaving sandwiches the warp threads with a weft thread. Warps, those long vertical threads attached to the loom, separate each column of beads.

Building a Loom

Looms can be purchased from bead and craft stores or on the Internet, or you can easily construct one yourself. A loom that can handle warps at least 36" long is required if you are going to make split-loom neckpieces. Bracelets require a loom 12" or longer.

Warps are the anchoring threads that run the length of the loom. The weft is the thread you string a needle and beads onto.

Construct the loom with two end boards nailed to a center board (1" x 8" stock works fine). Fasten a spring across the top as a warp separator.

String the warp threads onto your loom using nylon or silk thread. Some people prefer to use a slightly heavier warp thread than weft, though this is not necessary. Remember that the width of the finished piece will change depending on the size of thread used for the warps.

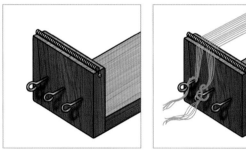

1. Eyehooks used to hold warp threads   2. Single warps being tied on in groups

For projects in which you will be taking the warps off and re-tying them back onto the loom, like some split-loom necklaces, use eyehooks on the end boards (1). Make the warp threads at least 42" for split-loom necklaces. Tie groups of four to ten warp threads onto the hooks with two overhand knots (2).

For projects that do not require taking off and re-tying warps, a cleat, which is available at hardware stores, can be used (3).

3. Cleat used to hold warp threads

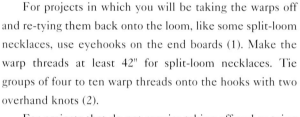

This method uses one continuous warp thread rather than many single threads. Wrap your warp threads around the cleat on each end of the loom (4). For bracelets and tapestries, a continuous warp thread is recommended. A continuous warp can be used just as easily with eyehooks (5).

String your warp threads onto the loom taut enough so there is a small but definite springy bounce when you push gently on them. They

4. Continuous warp wrapped onto cleat

should not sag at all, nor should they be tightly pluckable. Take care to insure that the tension is consistent among all the warps.

Depending on where your eyehooks or cleat are located, you may tighten the warps by sliding bead tube containers between the board and the warps, above where they are tied onto the loom (6).

5. Continuous warp wrapped onto cleat   6. Warps tightened with bead tubes

TECHNIQUES

Basic Loom Weaving

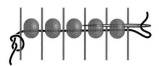

1. In these illustrations, the warp threads are orange, and the weft thread is black. Begin by tying your weft onto the left most warp with an overhand knot that you will eventually remove. Leave a tail at least 5" long to weave in and tie off later.

Position your weft thread under all the warps and upon it and string enough beads for one row. Push the beads up in between the warps, so that each bead has a warp thread on its left and its right side. Weave back through each bead, passing your needle above the warps. The weft will sandwich the warp threads.

If you are left-handed, it may be easier to tie your thread on the right-most warp, and work right to left.

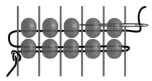

2. Tie off excess thread by wrapping it around warps, passing it through beads, and hiding it within beads. (The black weft has been changed to yellow so you can follow the tying off path.)
When you have finished weaving, use the method shown here to remove warps and tie them off.

Follow the yellow thread path. When a path of at least one full "circle" has been made with the thread (two circles is more secure), clip the excess thread as close to the right side of the last bead as possible. The end of the excess thread will be hidden inside the bead.

If you are making fringe out of the warp thread (as on the bottom of split-loom necklaces), string your fringe beads onto your warp, add a stop bead, bring your needle back up through the fringe beads, and work the end of that warp into the beadwork as shown above.

3. Tie off excess thread by wrapping it around warps, passing it through beads, and hiding it within beads. (The black weft has been changed to yellow so you can follow the tying off path.)
When you have finished weaving, use the method shown here to remove warps and tie them off.

Follow the yellow thread path. When a path of at least one full "circle" has been made with the thread (two circles is more secure), clip the excess thread as close to the right side of the last bead as possible. The end of the excess thread will be hidden inside the bead.

If you are making fringe out of the warp thread (as on the bottom of split-loom necklaces), string your fringe beads onto your warp, add a stop bead, bring your needle back up through the fringe beads, and work the end of that warp into the beadwork as shown above.

Decreasing Row Width on the Left Side

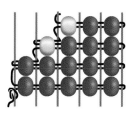

When decreasing the width of your loomwork on the left side, the weft thread must find its way to the left of the bead that begins each row. In other words, it must be in the same left-side position it is for non-decreasing rows. A yellow bead begins each decreased row.

Follow the path of the weft thread, wrapping it around the warp to the left of the bead that begins each row.

Increasing Row Width on the Left Side

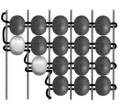

To increase the width of your loomwork on the left, the weft thread must find its way to the left of the bead that begins each row. In other words, the weft thread must be in the same left-side position it is for non-increasing rows. A yellow bead begins each increased row.

Follow the path of the weft thread, wrapping it around the warp to the left of the bead that begins each row.

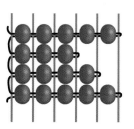

Decreasing and increasing on the right side is no different from straight weaving.

CONTRIBUTING ARTISTS

Robin Atkins began her work as a studio artist in the early 1980s. A nationally known bead artist, instructor, and speaker, her beadwork includes framed, sculptural and wearable pieces. Her work was selected for the cover of *500 Beaded Objects* (Lark Books, 2004) and has won awards in several competitions. She is the author of six books published by Tiger Press, including *One Bead at a Time* and *Beaded Treasures*. She co-authored Beaded Embellishments (Interweave Press, 2002), and has contributed to many books and magazines related to beading, quilting, and paper arts. The primary focus in Robin's books and workshops is the exploration of creativity and the development of personal style. In addition to her passion for bead art, Robin enjoys writing poems, creating handmade books, and painting. www.robinatkins.com

Thom Atkins has worked in many mediums, including paint, stained glass, fabric, beads, and clay and bronze sculpture. Having been introduced to beads in the 1970s, he returned to them in 2002, using the art quilt as a canvas. He began a search for balance between beads and cloth, where each has an equal voice in the composition. His love of flowers and landscapes inspires his vivid, bead-encrusted art quilts. He lives and works in Santa Cruz, Ca, and travels nationwide to teach. His work appears in *500 Beaded Objects* (Lark Books, 2004), *The Art of Beaded Beads* (Lark Books, 2006), *Beaded Embellishments* (Interweave Press, 2002), and *Innovative Fabric Imagery* (C&T Publishing, 2007). www.thomatkins.com

Paulette Baron is best known for creating three-dimensional sculptural beadwork. She teaches in the Washington, D.C. area, as well as at national bead shows and stores throughout the country. Her beadwork appears in *Beading with the Brick Stitch* (Interweave Press, 2001) and the Japanese publication *The Best Collection of Beadweaving Stitches by 9 American Bead Artists*. She has received national acclaim for both her beaded creatures and for her *Pinwheel Garden* necklace. www.paulettebaron.com

Frieda Bates is best known for her split-loom necklaces, namely the pottery designs featured in *The New Beadwork* (Harry N. Abrams, 1992). She lives her life surrounded by the beauty of New Mexico and an enormous bead and bead art collection. Nature and the southwest are her inspirations. She began beading in 1963, and has a driving passion for making gorgeous pieces out of specks of color. Her work has appeared in numerous magazines, books, and galleries. www.pvtnetworks.net/~fbates

Joan Reeder Babcock is an award-winning jewelry designer, teacher, and author who lives in Santa Fe, New Mexico. Joan has been creating jewelry and fiber art since 1988. Her unique style of fiber, bead, and metal jewelry, highlighting the technique of "Cavandoli" knotting, has been featured in Ornament and Beadwork magazines. She has been teaching nationally since 2004 and is the author of *Micro-Macramé Jewelry, Tips & Techniques for Knotting with Beads* (Joan Babcock Designs, 2005). www.joanbabcock.com

Ilene Combs Blanco stumbled into the beading industry in 1990 when she was hired to manage Beadworks of Sacramento. Networking with many of the industry leaders, instructors, and importers, Ilene quickly discovered that the diversity of the industry satisfied her creative interests. She established classes in Sacramento and trained many individuals who have since gone on to open stores and teach. Ilene opened one of the first full-service retail bead stores in Alabama, Bama Beads, in 1995, and a second location, Bella Beads, in Huntsville. Her wholesale company, International Jewelry & Beads, Inc. (California), supplies beads nationwide, and is known for its unique gemstone selection, full-service trunk shows, and innovative marketing bead programs for bead stores.

Inspired by the natural world, **Rebecca Brown-Thompson** draws on her background in horticulture and scientific illustration to create her dazzling beadwork. When she mastered the art of bead embroidery, it quickly took precedence over all of her

Fun at the Beach
by Kristy Nijenkamp
Lampwork and silver

other pursuits. She received "Best in Show" in *Bead and Button*'s 2001 exhibition. Her work is also featured in many books and magazines. She currently resides in New Zealand and was featured in Stitch: *Contemporary New Zealand Textile Artists* (Random House, 2006). She is the author of *Rebellious Beads: Advanced 3 Dimensional Beading* (Author House, 2006).
www.rbrown.co.nz

Jean Campbell is a fine artist who's been immersed in beads since 1990. She is the founding editor of *Beadwork* magazine and has written and edited numerous books, including *The Beader's Companion*, *Getting Started Stringing Beads*, *Beaded Weddings*, and *The Art of Beaded Beads*. Jean is cofounder of Shiny Bright Objects, a home-based bead party business, and teaches off-loom beading and metal clay workshops throughout the United States. She lives in Minneapolis, Minnesota, where she can be reached at jeanc@shinybrightobjects.com.

Cheryl Cobern-Browne gave up a nursing career in 1990 to move into the field of beadwork. Since then she's immersed herself in the craft's many facets, including designing, teaching, lecturing and the ownership of a bead shop. Formerly director of The Bead Museum in Glendale, Arizona, Cheryl now leads international Beadventure workshops. Her world travel and guest teacher itinerary is available on the Beadventure website.
www.beadventure.info

Having worked in the medium since 1968, Jeannette Cook is a nationally recognized bead artist and instructor and is well known for her company Beady Eyed Women. Teaching is a passion. She has lectured and taught beading techniques and bead design workshops at many of the nation's bead stores, societies and national shows since the 1980s. She is the co-author *The Beady-Eyed Woman*'s book series (Interweave Press, 2006), the author of *Beading with Peyote Stitch* (Interweave Press, 2007), and her work has been featured in leading bead magazines.
www.beadyeyedwomen.com

SaraBeth Cullinan has always been obsessed with color. As a child she longed for the crayon box with 120 colors and that obsession has carried over into beads. With a degree in Veterinary Technology and an extensive background in dance, SaraBeth combines her love of color, nature, and movement into her art. She is a frequent contributor to *Beadwork* and *Stringing* magazines and her work has been published in a variety of beading books.

Carol Cypher, author of *Hand Felted Jewelry and Beads: 25 Artful Designs* (Inerweave Press, 2006), *Mastering Beadwork: A Comprehensive Guide to Off-Loom Techniques* (Interweave Press, 2006), and *How We Felt* (Interweave Press, 2007) teaches beadwork and feltmaking and is known for her provocative pairing of these two crafts. Carol's work appears in several books and international magazines. She enjoys a reputation as an enthusiastic, knowledgeable, and generous teacher and artist.
www.carolcypher.com

Jamie Cloud Eakin is a professional bead artist, teacher, and perpetual student of her craft. For over a decade, her original designs have been collected by discriminating buyers and by fine galleries across the United States. She has won numerous awards for her beadwork and has been featured in various publications. Jamie is the author of *Beading with Cabochons* (Lark Books, 2005).
www.StudioJamie.com

Art Deco
by Heidi Kummli
Chrysocolla, glass beads, brass stamping,
bead embroidery and loom weaving
Photograph by Heidi Kummli

Wendy Ellsworth is a seed bead artist living in Bucks County, Pennsylvania. Beading since 1970, her signature *SeaForms* can be found in numerous private collections and museums. Her beadwork has also been featured in many books and periodicals as well as in select gallery exhibitions. She teaches nationally and internationally and received a 2003 Fellowship from the Pennsylvania Council on the Arts. www.ellsworthstudios.com

Marcia DeCoster has enjoyed teaching nationally since the early 1990s. Her designs are component oriented, as she likes to play with variations in design and color in small pieces, which are then joined to create fabulous jewelry. Her work has been published in *The Complete Guide to Beading Techniques* (Beadwork Books 2001), *The Art and Elegance of Bead Weaving* (Search Press, 2002), and *Bead and Button* and *Beadwork* magazine.
www.marciadecoster.com

Artist, musician, and color expert **Margie Deeb** is the author of several beading books, including the popular *The Beader's Guide to Color* (Watson-Guptill, 2004), *Beading Her Image* (Minoa, 2006), and *Out On a Loom* (Minoa, 1999). Her passion for color and movement is the driving force in all her creations. Her work has appeared in galleries, shows, leading magazines, and books, including *500 Beaded Objects* (Lark Books, 2004). She teaches color courses across the country and her free monthly color column, *Margie's Muse*, is available on her Web site. She produces a graphically enhanced podcast, *Margie Deeb's Color Celebration*, available on iTunes. Visit Margie's website for her books, patterns, jewelry, inspiration, and more information.
www.MargieDeeb.com.

Margo C. Field "discovered" beads in 1990 after retiring from a career in hospital pharmacy. Later, she opened Poppy Field Bead Company in Albuquerque, NM. Her work has been featured in many publications and she has received numerous awards. Margo's work is inspired by nature and her passion for flowers and foliage. She teaches workshops at her store and across the US.
www.poppyfield.com

Diane Guzman, a dollmaker and quilter, frequently employs beads in her artwork. The beaded footstool is one of a few beaded objects she has made while taking a break from her other work. Her dolls have been featured in *Art Doll Quarterly* magazine and she has shown her quilts in various shows.
www.dianesstudio.com.

Mary Hicklin, a lifelong beader, started Virgo Moon in 1990 as a service to those who like herself, believe you can't wear too many beads. She is a recovering software engineer and unrepentant sea kayaker. Her work has been featured in *Ornament* magazine and in several jewelry art books, including *The Beader's Guide to Color* (Watson-Guptill, 2004).
www.virgomoon.com

Lisa Niven Kelly has been teaching wire/bead work for fifteen years, putting students "in charge of the wire" and making them laugh. Her passion lies with mixing modern and classical techniques in both metal and glass. Lisa has been a finalist in many national competitions and is a regular contributor to many top magazines. She currently resides in the San Francisco Bay area where she manages her online shop, which features tools, kits, and online classes.
www.beaducation.com
www.lisanivenkelly.com

Heidi Kummli has been beading full time since 1990 when she started her company, Free Spirit Collection. She has written several articles and her work has been published in many publications and books. Heidi has won numerous awards for her beadwork over the past sixteen years including the 2003 Saul Bell Design Award. Heidi is co-author of *The Art of Bead Embroidery* with Sherry Serafini (Kalmbach Publishing, 2007). She currently lives off the grid on twelve acres in the Colorado Rockies where she finds inspiration from her natural surroundings.
www.freespiritcollection.com

Karen Lewis discovered the medium of polymer clay in the late 1980s and her life took a dramatic turn. In her words, "My life has not been the same since; the clay and I developed a rapport and by the end of the sixth month of discovery I thought I'd reinvented the wheel!" She has produced five instructional videos and her work appears in trade magazines, books, museum collections, and is shown worldwide. She was a featured guest artist on the Learning Channel's *Simply Style* in the show about the Smithsonian Artrain (1998).
www.klewexpressions.com

Kristy Nijenkamp has been fascinated with melting glass since her childhood glimpses of glass blowing in Venice. She sells her work at private and artisan shows and by appointment. She has served many terms on the board of the Atlanta Southern Flames, a chapter of the International Society of Glass Beadmakers and continually supports new artists in the hot glass field, especially concerning studio safety and health. Kristy's passion is creating custom, one-of-a-kind pieces of jewelry, or art incorporating glass, metal and wood. Her work is featured in *One Big Beautiful Bead* (Lark Books, 2007) and *The Beader's Guide to Color* (Watson-Guptill, 2004). She can be reached at nijenkamp@bellsouth.net.

Kimberley Price has been designing jewelry for over two decades. Her work includes stringing, silver chainmaking ,and beadwork, but her passion is for beaded sculptures. Kim's style has been influenced by the whimsy of her parents' extensive folk art collection, and life with her young family. Her work has been seen in international competition and numerous beadwork publications. Her beaded *Old Woman in the Shoe* was a finalist in Beadwork magazine's traveling Embellished Shoe exhibit and her Princess and the Pea Purse was included in the *Caravan Beads Myths and Folktales of the World* book (Caravan Beads, 2000) showcasing their Second Delica Challenge entries.
kim.price@sympatico.ca

Tracey Rodgerson has a background in graphic design. Interested in many contemporary crafts, she began making lampworked glass beads in 1995. After seeing a piece by Sherry Serafini in 2003, she was inspired to try, and has fallen in love with, bead embroidery. Her inspiration is the beads themselves, the encouragement that comes from her family and friends, and her passion to create. Tracey and her cat live in Swartz Creek, Michigan.
www.purplecreekbeads.com

Elizabeth Ann Scarborough, a lifelong beader, draws her inspiration from folk art and from the colors and textures of the materials themselves. In 2005, her Egyptian-style crystal collar was a finalist in the Swarovski Create Your Style Cultural Fusion contest. Additionally, her *Librarian Storyteller* necklace appeared in *Beadwork* magazine, and her *Lovely Lacy Lavender Lavaliere*

appeared in *The Beader's Guide to Color* (Watson-Guptill, 2004). She is the author of *Beadtime Stories*, a pattern book.
www.eascarborough.com

Sherry Serafini is a beadwork artist who has been creating beaded art since 1997. This methodical and meditative form of art is a rich counterpoint to a society of instant gratification. She lectures and teaches throughout the U.S. and her work has been published widely in leading books and magazines. Sherry has received numerous awards for her beaded art, including a Jurors Merit Award in the Bead International, People's Choice Award in the Bead Dreams competition, and Best of Pennsylvania Artisans award. She is regular on the *Beads, Baubles and Jewels* show sponsored by Firemountain Gems and featured in *Bead&Button* magazine. Steven Tyler of Aerosmith has worn her work onstage and commissioned her beadwork for promotional material. Other fans include pro golfer Michelle Wie, Melissa Etheridge, and Fergie of the Black Eyed Peas. Sherry is co-author of *The Art of Bead Embroidery* (Kalmbach, 2007) with Heidi Kummli
www.serafinibeadedjewelry.com

Carol Zilliacus is a fine artist with an unusual slant on polymer clay. She originated tapestry techniques, (introduced at *Making History*, the first national conference of the National Clay Guild in 1997), which is a way of portraying tapestries, crewel work, and fabric in polymer clay. Tapestry techniques take clay into the realm of fine art, allowing her to design sheets of polymer clay with many blended colors that have a variety of value and hue. An award-winning Maryland artist whose work is exhibited nationally in American Craft Council shows as well as Washington D.C. area galleries, she has been featured in newspaper articles, art books, videos, and TV programs. In March 2004 Carol was invited to participate in the exhibition An Exploration of Polymer Clay at the Kentucky Museum of Arts & Design in Louisville.
www.carolszilliacusartist.com

Chrysocolla Chrysalis
Necklace and earring set by Elizabeth Ann Scarborough
Chrysocolla from the Baghdad copper mine, fancy glass beads, copper, turquoise, and malachite

SUPPLIES & RESOURCES

Radiant Sun Earrings (pages 28–29)
All materials:
• *Fire Mountain Gems*

Lagoon Beaded Belt (pages 30–32)
Pewter finding, charms, beads, sterling rounds, fire polish, Czech glass:
• Shipwreck Beads
Russian cut beads:
• Rings & Things
Crystals:
• Beyond Beadery Fire Mountain Gems

Mermaid's Collar (pages 33–35)
Headpins, crimp covers, beads:
• Fire Mountain Gems
Sterling clasp:
• Bella Beads
Pale teal flat-pointed oval beads:
• vintage from the author's personal collection

Clay Disk Pendant (pages 36–37)
Clay disks:
• Mike Stedman
Beads:
• Fire Mountain Gems

Ceramic Pendant (pages 60–61)
Jump rings, headpin, crimps, glass beads:
• Rio Grande
24kt gold plated seed beads:
• Out On A Whim
Decorative connector ring:
• Rishashay
Handmade ceramic beads:
• Some Enchanted Beading

Constructivist Bracelet (pages 62–63)
Beads, thread, needle:
• Fire Mountain Gems

Draped Troy Multi-strand Necklace (pages 64–65)
Beads:
• Fire Mountain Gems
12-strand vermeil clasp:
• MargieDeeb.com

Minoan Embroidered Pendant (pages 66–68)
Cabochons and neck ring:
• Rio Grande

Beads:
• Fire Mountain Gems
Ultraseude:
• Denver Fabrics

Multi-strand Seed Bead Bracelet (pages 85–86)
Beads:
• Storm Cloud Trading
3-hole clasp:
• Rishashay

Festival of Fringe Necklace (pages 87–88)
Beads and clasp:
• Fire Mountain Gems
Yellow disk beads:
• vintage from the author's personal collection

Collar of Glass & Light (pages 89–90)
24k gold-plated seed beads:
• Out On A Whim
Glass dagger beads:
• Copper Coyote
Vermeil clasp:
• Rishashay

Blended Multi-strand Necklace (pages 91–94)
Beads and clasp:
• Fire Mountain Gems
• Shipwreck Beads

Tuscan Headpin Earrings (pages 107–108)
Chandelier components, beads, headpins:
• ArtBeads.com
9-hole earring hoops:
• Rio Grande

Crystal & Lampwork Pendant (pages 109–111)
Focal lampwork bead:
• Comparable bead available from Eclectica or individual bead artists and bead stores
Crystal Beads:
• Beyond Beadery
Silver bail:
• Rio Grande

Rainforest Cascade Necklace (pages 112–113)
Beads, patina brass leaves, cones:
• Fire Mountain Gems

Lavender Rose Brooch (pages 114–116)
Ultraseude:
• Denver Fabrics
Dichroic cabochon:
• Comparable cabochons available from Eclectica or individual bead artists and bead stores
Beads and pin back:
• Fire Mountain Gems

Fancy Dangle Bracelet (pages 132–133)
Beads, headpins, jump rings, beading wire:
• Fire Mountain Gems

Seed Bead Swag Necklace (pages 134–136)
Seed beads, Delicas and Swarovski crystals:
• Fire Mountain Gems
Beyond Beadery Silver findings, fire polish beads, and beading wire:
• Fire Mountain Gems
Czech crystal rondelles and Cultura pearls:
• Shipwreck Beads
Sterling silver barn owl toggle clasp:
• NeoMythica (Margaret Braet)

Sparkling Draped Loop Collar (pages 137–139)
Beads and clasp:
• Fire Mountain Gems

Multi-strand Pendant & Tassel (pages 140–145)
Handmade beads:
• Karen Ovington
Seed beads:
• Caravan Beads
Rhodonite and rose quartz:
• J&V Jewelry
• Fire Mountain Gems
Grossular garnet lozenges and tiny tourmaline shapes:
• Wraps Stones & Things
Grossular garnet faceted cylinders, sterling spacers, beads, and cones:
• Anil Kumar
Grossular garnet faceted rounds:
• Lan's Beads (800) 955-9992 or Fire Mountain Gems
Sterling wire:
• Rio Grande

Hematite and glass beads embroidered on Sensuede by Margie Deeb. Silver clasp

ONLINE & MAIL ORDER SOURCES

Artbeads.com
(253) 857-2372
www.artbeads.com
Seed beads, semi-precious stone beads,
Swarovski, resin, shell, components, and findings

Beads Galore
(480) 921-3949
beadsgalore.com
Seed beads, semi-precious stone beads,
Swarovski, and ethnic beads

Bella Beads
(256) 534-3949
bellabeadsandjewelry.com
Wide variety of beads, including Delicas and
seed beads, pearls, gemstones, findings, books,
magazines, tools

Beyond Beadery
(800) 840-5548
www.beyondbeadery.com
Delicas and seed beads, various sized beads and
findings, beading tools, books, and videos

Caravan Beads
(800) 230-8941
www.caravanbeads.com
Delicas and seed beads, various sized beads and
findings

Copper Coyote Beads
(502) 722-8440
www.coppercoyote.com
Beads, books, videos

MargieDeeb.com
www.margiedeeb.com
Clasps, bead patterns, color wheels,
tapestry rods

Denver Fabrics
www.denverfabrics.com
Fabric

Eclectica
(262) 641-0910
www.eclecticabeads.com
Vintage beads, artists' beads, dichroic glass

Fire Mountain Gems
(800) 355-2137
www.firemountaingems.com
Wide variety of beads, including Delicas and
seed beads, gemstones, findings, beading tools,
books and videos

General Bead
(415) 621-8187
www.genbead.com
Delicas and seed beads, semi-precious stone
bead and findings

J&V Jewelry
(213) 489-9219
Semi-precious stones, freshwater pearls, natural
beads

Anil Kumar
(510) 498-8455
Silver, gold, spacers, semi-precious beads,
precious beads (sells at gem shows only;
no retail store)

Lan's Beads
(800) 955-9992
www.lansbeads.com
Semi-precious beads, fresh and saltwater pearls

NeoMythica (Margaret Braet)
(913) 485-9075
www.neomythica.com
Toggles, balls, components

Out On A Whim
(800) 232-3111
www.whimbeads.com
Delicas and seed beads, various sized beads and
findings, beading tools, books and videos

Karen Ovington
www.karenovington@sbcglobal.net
(773) 764-5200
Handmade glass beads

Pacific Silverworks
(805) 641-1394
www.pacificsilverworks.com
Findings, clasps, and components

Rings & Things
(800) 366-2156
www.rings-things.com
Beads, findings, charms, cord, polymer clay,
Swarovski crystal beads and prisms, Czech glass
beads, jewelry display items

Sparkling draped loop collar necklaces by Margie Deeb

Rhodochrosite cabbed pendant
and earrings
Glass beads and pearls,
rhodonite, rose quartz
Necklace and earrings by
Elizabeth Ann Scarborough

Rio Grande
(800) 545-6566
Wide variety of beads, including Delicas and
seed beads, gemstones, findings, beading tools,
packaging, books and videos

Rishashay
(800) 517-3311
www.rishashay.com
Unusual findings and clasps

Scottsdale Bead Supply
(480) 945-5988
www.scottsdalebead.com
Findings and clasps

Shipwreck Beads
(360) 754-2323
www.shipwreck-beads.com
Wide variety of seed beads, including Delicas
and Tohos, gemstones, findings, beading tools,
books and videos

Some Enchanted Beading
www.someenchantedbeading.com
Handmade ceramic beads from Africa.
The company provides and sustains
employment for African women in Kenya.

Mike Stedman
(404) 915-5743
mstedman@sprintmail.com

Stormcloud Trading
(651) 645-0343
www.beadstorm.com
Delicas and seed beads

Star's Clasps
(800) 207-2805
www.starsclasps.com
Hand-crafted clasps

Wraps Stones & Things
(415) 863-4953
www.beadsnclasps.com
Clasps and semi-precious beads

DELICA CROSS-REFERENCE

DB-001: 10, 27, 62, 81, 83, 120, 122, 129, 131
DB-010: 39, 62, 74, 75, 77, 98, 119, 121, 122, 129, 137
DB-011: 25, 50, 51, 56, 105
DB-022: 43, 50, 54, 98
DB-027: 98, 100
DB-031: 18, 21, 27, 28, 39, 42, 43, 46, 48, 49, 50, 53, 54, 57, 59, 64, 73, 77, 83, 84, 85, 89, 137
DB-032: 25, 45, 83, 89
DB-038: 57
DB-040: 36, 43
DB-043: 84
DB-045: 21, 25
DB-051: 19
DB-052: 77
DB-053: 50, 54, 130
DB-054: 48, 56
DB-057: 19, 25, 57, 71, 75, 103
DB-059: 124
DB-062: 98, 126
DB-063: 77, 122
DB-066: 130
DB-067: 56
DB-068: 48, 71
DB-069: 42, 47, 48, 124
DB-070: 129
DB-072: 106
DB-073: 21, 100, 106, 112, 127, 132
DB-074: 126, 130
DB-076: 19, 71, 77, 87
DB-077: 71
DB-078: 25, 33, 97, 106, 119
DB-079: 25
DB-080: 17
DB-081: 27
DB-082: 18
DB-083: 18, 19
DB-085, 19
DB-098: 42, 100, 127
DB-099: 58
DB-100: 19
DB-101: 48, 50, 124
DB-103: 103
DB-105: 45, 77
DB-106: 49, 83
DB-108: 54, 96
DB-113: 19, 89
DB-115: 21
DB-116: 27, 43, 47
DB-121: 43
DB-124: 56
DB-125: 137
DB-1301: 97
DB-1302: 21, 27, 45, 51, 54, 56, 71, 77, 80, 81, 100, 103, 123

DB-131: 25
DB-1312: 71, 84, 98, 126
DB-1340: 122
DB-1345: 30, 106, 122, 126, 130
DB-1363: 103
DB-1371: 127
DB-1405: 105, 106
DB-1413: 81, 98, 106
DB-1414: 54, 71, 112, 119
DB-1451: 43, 45, 47, 48, 54, 105, 123
DB-1452: 58
DB-1453: 58
DB-1454: 25, 27, 54, 104
DB-1456: 62, 81, 124, 129
DB-1457: 18, 54, 124
DB-1459: 45
DB-1471: 19
DB-1473: 19

DB-1475: 41
DB-1478: 45, 123
DB-1479: 17, 19, 83, 103
DB-1480: 81
DB-1483: 54
DB-1484: 27, 83
DB-1490: 30, 71, 101, 102, 104, 120, 127
DB-1491: 84, 106, 119, 122, 127
DB-1492: 103
DB-1495: 59
DB-1497: 80, 101, 102, 105, 131
DB-1500: 18, 27, 48, 71
DB-1502: 41
DB-1506: 25, 33
DB-151: 84, 120

DB-152: 101
DB-1520: 83, 129
DB-1522: 104
DB-1523: 54
DB-1526: 54, 59, 100, 103, 104
DB-1530: 54, 71, 101, 126, 130
DB-1532: 27, 128
DB-1536: 25, 109, 119
DB-1537: 17, 27, 50, 75
DB-157: 124
DB-159: 106, 127
DB-160: 54, 56, 57, 71, 75, 84, 87, 97, 98, 105, 119, 122, 127
DB-161: 21, 46, 75, 84, 97, 98, 120, 122, 127
DB-163: 129
DB-165: 25, 30, 42, 60, 87, 97, 101, 119, 120
DB-166: 77, 119

DB-167: 71, 74, 75, 122
DB-169: 25, 57, 58, 76, 77, 98, 119, 120, 126, 129
DB-170: 98, 100
DB-171: 71
DB-172: 120
DB-174: 84, 87, 98, 100, 119, 120, 126, 127, 130
DB-178: 122
DB-181: 27, 45
DB-182: 46
DB-183: 45
DB-200: 58, 59, 74, 76, 77
DB-201: 75, 80, 81, 97, 122, 127
DB-203: 17, 19, 28, 39, 41, 42, 43, 35, 46, 48, 49, 50, 53, 56,

59, 60, 62, 98, 105, 124, 129, 132, 134
DB-204: 48
DB-205: 48, 77, 83, 124
DB-206: 71, 100
DB-207: 75, 101, 129
DB-208: 41, 46, 56, 85
DB-209: 19
DB-210: 10, 49, 120, 127
DB-211: 104
DB-214: 98, 100
DB-215: 30, 39, 54, 57, 70, 121
DB-217: 54, 58, 80
DB-218: 47, 71, 83, 123
DB-232: 21, 57, 75
DB-233: 10, 19, 21, 41, 42, 48, 56, 57, 59, 71, 76, 84, 97, 98, 100, 104, 105, 106, 107, 119, 120, 123, 126, 127, 129
DB-235: 17, 21, 59, 100, 120
DB-236: 21, 71, 75, 127, 140
DB-237: 25, 58, 71, 75, 109, 119
DB-238: 39, 84
DB-240: 17, 18, 25, 41, 71, 76, 80
DB-243: 58
DB-244: 59, 60, 127
DB-245: 74, 106, 120
DB-247: 73, 87, 105, 106, 112, 122, 126, 130
DB-248: 98, 120, 140
DB-249: 25, 106
DB-253: 49
DB-254: 27, 28, 50, 62
DB-257: 25, 49, 58, 71, 106
DB-266: 58
DB-271: 62
DB-272: 27, 41, 56, 74, 129
DB-274: 25, 27, 59, 70, 74, 97, 101, 104
DB-275: 25, 27
DB-277: 39, 41, 43, 46, 71
DB-278: 27, 50
DB-280: 48, 51, 119
DB-281: 54, 58, 73, 84, 112, 132
DB-283: 83
DB-285: 25, 48, 50, 58, 71, 101
DB-287: 9, 48, 58, 102, 107, 140
DB-295: 59, 75, 129, 131
DB-296: 21, 75
DB-301: 19, 21, 27, 39, 41, 43, 58, 62, 77, 109, 120, 129
DB-310: 41, 42, 43, 46, 48, 50, 54, 57, 58, 59, 62, 66, 76, 77, 83, 87, 91, 97, 106, 119, 120, 123, 129, 131, 134
DB-311: 45, 80, 81, 103
DB-312: 27, 43, 47, 48, 77, 81, 101
DB-318: 27

Purple Python
by Kristy Nijenkamp
Amethyst, black onyx, lampwork,
silver on memory wire

DB-322: 85, 107
DB-327: 85, 103
DB-331: 9, 21, 28, 46, 74, 83, 84, 90
DB-352: 54, 62, 81, 100, 122, 129, 134, 140
DB-353: 39, 48, 50, 51, 54, 81, 100, 101, 104
DB-354: 104
DB-355: 104
DB-357: 58
DB-361: 18, 43, 45, 75, 90, 91, 100, 106
DB-371: 25, 80, 96, 101, 105, 114
DB-372: 56, 103
DB-373: 43, 45
DB-374: 66, 85, 101, 103, 127
DB-375: 36, 39, 56, 104
DB-376: 19, 27, 41, 43, 54, 80, 85, 105, 106, 124
DB-377: 25, 27, 41, 45, 46, 48, 105, 106, 124
DB-378: 39, 48, 74, 76
DB-381: 18, 19, 27, 58, 102, 105, 107, 114, 124
DB-388: 45, 57, 80
DB-461: 27, 28, 46, 48, 50, 134, 137
DB-605: 46
DB-610: 21, 46, 73, 127
DB-621: 9, 27, 46, 50, 54, 60, 64
DB-622: 19, 41, 103, 105, 106
DB-629: 43, 81, 114, 124
DB-651: 10, 21, 27, 39, 41, 42, 56, 57, 58, 66, 71, 74, 75, 76, 77, 80, 97, 100, 104, 105, 120
DB-653: 41, 77, 105
DB-654: 21, 27, 43, 46, 48, 51, 71, 75, 77, 91, 105, 119, 129
DB-655: 76
DB-656: 74
DB-661: 106, 126, 127
DB-663: 25, 27, 71, 105
DB-682: 96
DB-683: 46, 84
DB-684: 71, 74, 105
DB-687: 41, 56, 74
DB-688: 119
DB-689: 45
DB-690: 75, 107, 129
DB-691: 25, 53, 75
DB-694: 17, 25
DB-695: 43, 124
DB-696: 46, 74
DB-703: 21, 56, 71, 84, 97
DB-705: 83, 87, 89, 97, 100, 105, 126
DB-707: 48, 57, 59, 76, 80, 83, 89
DB-714: 89
DB-721: 74
DB-722: 21
DB-726: 42, 80, 81
DB-727: 57, 80, 97, 119
DB-728: 49

DB-729: 42, 83, 100, 104
DB-730: 49, 50, 74, 76, 101, 105, 131
DB-731: 54, 58, 103
DB-734: 21, 27, 51, 56, 103, 124, 134
DB-742: 21, 48, 77, 100, 104, 126, 129
DB-743: 58
DB-744: 57, 119
DB-745: 57, 58, 87
DB-746: 25, 57, 71, 98, 100, 105
DB-748: 77
DB-749: 10, 21, 83, 120, 134
DB-751: 21, 59, 77
DB-752: 120
DB-754: 27, 77, 112
DB-757: 21, 59, 77, 129
DB-759: 109
DB-760: 102, 120
DB-761: 62, 84
DB-762: 62, 74, 77, 80
DB-764: 27, 48, 58, 71, 74, 77, 81, 85, 103, 105, 106, 129
DB-769: 27, 48
DB-772: 103
DB-773: 41, 45, 49, 56, 58, 66,

Jamie Cloud Eakin
Yellow agate, dendritic opal, citrine

81, 84, 103
DB-776: 58, 80, 81, 97, 105, 112
DB-777: 102, 103, 104, 107, 114
DB-778: 127
DB-779: 80
DB-781: 21, 43, 45, 50, 56, 81, 98, 104
DB-785: 71
DB-787: 25, 104, 121
DB-788: 25, 33, 36, 56, 109
DB-792: 25, 56, 62
DB-793: 25, 33, 39, 56, 97, 101, 121
DB-794: 43
DB-795: 39, 56, 77
DB-798: 33, 39, 42, 54, 83, 100, 103
DB-799: 43, 56, 114, 124
DB-800: 10, 18, 53, 120, 127
DB-817: 46
DB-852: 80
DB-854: 127
DB-859: 25
DB-860: 120
DB-861: 80, 101, 104
DB-862: 43, 53
DB-877: 98, 100

DB-878: 33
DB-881: 54, 58, 75
DB-883: 25, 41, 48, 50, 104
DB-901: 43, 98, 100, 106, 122, 128
DB-902: 54, 75, 83
DB-904: 25, 77
DB-905: 66
DB-906: 17
DB-908: 25, 27, 104
DB-909: 73
DB-910: 84, 96, 101, 114, 129, 137, 140
DB-911: 71, 103, 140
DB-913: 21, 83
DB-914: 21, 54, 57, 59, 70, 98, 106, 127, 140
DB-915: 27, 36, 124
DB-917: 25, 54, 59, 77, 98, 100, 112, 120
DB-918: 25, 39, 109, 122
DB-919: 42, 46, 57, 59, 60, 62, 71, 83, 126, 129
DB-920: 30, 48, 54
DB-922: 45, 119
DB-923: 17, 21, 114
DB-924: 76

Tears of Coral
by Kristy Nijenkamp
Carved coral

GEMSTONE CROSS-REFERENCE

abalone: 72, 158

African brown rhyolite: 26

agate: 18, 21, 22, 24, 25, 26, 40, 41, 42, 47, 75, 77, 103, 124

amazonite: 24, 25, 26

amber: 19, 21, 22, 48, 75, 77, 84, 105, 120, 129

amethyst: 13, 17, 18, 21, 25, 30, 31, 39, 45, 124, 126

ametrine: 18

apatite: 24, 79

aquamarine: 24, 44

aventurine: 21, 22, 25, 26, 36, 102

black onyx: 22, 26, 131

blue agate: 18, 24, 25, 26

blue goldstone: 26

blue lace agate: 18, 41

carnelian: 13, 21, 22, 39, 41, 42, 75, 81, 84, 119, 162

chalcedony: 17, 19, 24, 40, 41, 42, 61, 75, 80, 109, 154

chrysocolla: 24, 26, 154, 181, 183

chrysoprase: 24, 25, 26

citrine: 13, 18, 19, 21, 22, 26, 43, 120, 129, 147, 162

clear quartz: 18

copper: 26, 27, 28, 36, 39, 43, 46, 50, 107, 108, 156, 183, 184

coral: 17, 21, 22, 27, 41, 47, 54, 73, 74, 105, 122, 129, 131, 189

feldspath: 26

fluorite: 18, 24, 159

freshwater pearls: 17, 18, 41, 47, 158, 185

garnet: 22, 44, 75, 119, 140, 184

gold: 9, 18, 21, 22, 26, 27, 28, 39, 42, 43, 45, 46, 47, 48, 49, 50, 52, 54, 57, 59, 60, 64, 73, 74, 75, 77, 83, 84, 85, 86, 89, 90, 91, 96, 103, 107, 108, 118, 123, 132

green agate: 24, 159

hematite: 21, 22, 26, 40, 84, 119, 120, 129, 131, 166

iolite: 18, 158

ivory: 17, 28, 39, 42, 43, 48, 49, 60, 124, 129

jade: 22, 24, 25, 27, 75, 109, 119

jasper: 26, 39, 40, 41, 42, 46, 51, 79, 100, 103, 105, 129, 131

labradorite: 18, 19

lapis lazuli: 24, 39, 42

lavender fluorite: 18

moonstone: 18, 19, 24, 27, 105, 129

mother-of-pearl: 17, 20, 124, 129, 158

obsidian: 13, 21, 22, 26

olivine: 26

onyx: 22, 25, 26, 39, 109, 131

peach moonstone: 105, 129

pearl: 17, 21, 24, 25, 31, 32, 74, 75, 80, 108, 124, 129, 134, 135, 136, 142

peridot: 13, 24, 25, 118, 119, 126

prehnite: 18, 24

quartz: 13, 18, 26, 39, 54, 79, 81, 120

rainbow calcite: 80

rainbow moonstone: 18, 19

red agate: 21, 22

red aventurine: 21, 22, 103

red coral: 21, 22, 129, 131, 153

red jade: 22

red jasper: 131

rhodonite: 47, 75, 105

rhyolite: 26, 105

rose quartz: 13, 18, 54, 120, 186

serpentine: 24, 26, 27, 80, 105

silver: 19, 21, 24, 25, 26, 27, 28, 30, 33, 35, 39, 42, 43, 45, 46, 54, 55, 57, 59, 64, 74, 75, 77, 81, 82, 83, 107, 109, 134, 140, 146, 156, 180, 182, 184, 185, 187

smokey quartz: 26, 136

sodalite: 24, 41, 80

stringing: 65, 75, 86, 110, 111, 133, 169-170, 171

sunstone: 22, 105

tanzanite: 18, 19, 27

tigereye: 21, 22, 26, 51, 129

topaz: 9, 19, 21, 44, 77

tourmaline: 13, 26

turquoise: 19, 25, 26, 38, 39, 52, 72, 73, 75, 89, 97, 99, 119, 131, 146, 151, 154, 165, 183

unakite: 26

PHOTO CREDITS

All designs, diagrams, artwork, and photographs produced by Margie Deeb except as otherwise specified throughout the book and below.

Shutterstock: 8 (top), 11, 17 (top right), 19 (top right), 20 (top right), 22 (bottom), 23 (top and bottom right), 24 (top right), 27 (top right), 28 (bottom), 30 (bottom), 33 (bottom), 36 (bottom), 39 (top right and second from bottom), 40 (bottom), 44 (right), 46 (top left), 49 (bottom and second from bottom), 54 (second and third from top), 66 (bottom), 70 (bottom right), 71 (third from top), 73 (top right and bottom left), 74 (all except necklace), 75 (all except necklace), 77 (top left), 78 (center), 80 (bottom and second from bottom), 81 (top left), 83 (all except necklace), 84 (center top and second from bottom), 87 (bottom), 91 (bottom), 96 (bottom), 97 (top and bottom left), 98 (top right and bottom left), 99 (right), 100 (all except earrings), 101 (all except bracelet), 102 (top right and bottom left), 103 (all except necklace), 104 (top and bottom left), 105 (all except necklace), 106 (all except necklace), 107 (bottom left), 109 (bottom), 112 (bottom left), 114 (bottom), 118 (top right and bottom left), 119 (all except necklace), 120 (all except necklace), 121 (top right and bottom left), 122 (all except necklace), 123 (top right and bottom left), 124 (bottom and second from bottom), 125 (top right), 126 (all except necklace), 127 (bottom and second and third from bottom), 128 (right), 129 (bottom right), 130 (all except necklace), 131 (top center and bottom left), 132 (bottom left), 134 (bottom), 137 (bottom), 140 (bottom), 150 (top), 151 (bottom), 153 (bottom), 154 (bottom), 155 (top), 156 (bottom), 157 (top), 158 (left), 161 (bottom), 162 (top), 163 (center, inside necklace), 164 (bottom), 167 (bottom)

Eyewire: 26 (middle), 126 (bottom)

ABOUT THE AUTHOR

Artist, musician, and color expert Margie Deeb is the author of several beading books, including the popular *The Beader's Guide to Color* (Watson-Guptill, 2004). She teaches color and beading courses across the country.

www.MargieDeeb.com

Photograpgh by Jim Perdue

INDEX